C000245200

A GARDENER'S GUIDE TO
500 FUCHSIAS

A GARDENER'S GUIDE TO
500 FUCHSIAS

Varieties for growing in hanging baskets and pots, hardy fuchsias, species fuchsias, unusual cultivars and Encliandras, with over 270 photographs

JOHN NICHOLASS

PHOTOGRAPHY BY PETER ANDERSON

southwater

This edition is published by Southwater
an imprint of Anness Publishing Ltd
Blaby Road, Wigston, Leicestershire LE18 4SE
info@anness.com

www.southwaterbooks.com
www.annesspublishing.com

If you like the images in this book and would
like to investigate using them for publishing,
promotions or advertising, please visit our website
www.practicalpictures.com for more information.

© Anness Publishing Ltd 2012

All rights reserved. No part of this publication may be
reproduced, stored in a retrieval system, or transmitted
in any way or by any means, electronic, mechanical,
photocopying, recording or otherwise, without the prior
written permission of the copyright holder.

A CIP catalogue record for this book
is available from the British Library.

Publisher: Joanna Lorenz
Senior Editor: Felicity Forster
Photographer: Peter Anderson
Designer: Lisa Tai
Cover Design: Nigel Partridge
Production Controller: Pirong Wang

Previously published as part of a larger volume,
The Gardener's Guide to Growing Fuchsias

PUBLISHER'S NOTE
Although the advice and information in this book are believed
to be accurate and true at the time of going to press, neither the
authors nor the publisher can accept any legal responsibility or
liability for any errors or omissions that may have been made nor
for any inaccuracies nor for any loss, harm or injury that comes
about from following instructions or advice in this book.

CONTENTS

Introduction

Fuchsias are superb summer-flowering plants. They are fast growing, come in a range of flower colours and sizes, and can be used in containers, hanging baskets and as summer bedding in the garden borders. They are also very easy to train into different shapes, the standard fuchsia being most familiar. More than 10,000 fuchsia cultivars have been introduced since the work of the first fuchsia hybridizers started in the early 19th century. Many of these have been lost over the years, but some have been continuously in commerce for more than 100 years, which is a good indicator that there is something special about them. Fuchsia nurseries introduce more than 300 new cultivars worldwide every year.

The original discovery of the genus Fuchsia was in the southern hemisphere, and the first record of the fuchsia in Western civilization was in the early 18th century. There are more than 100 identified fuchsia species found mainly in the southern hemisphere of the world. The majority are originally from South America, with most of the remainder found in Central America, Tahiti and New Zealand.

Top: The large double flower of 'Irene Sinton', with its blush-pink sepals, a full lilac-blue corolla and splashes of pink on the petals. The opening flower bud, sprinkled with raindrops, is about to reveal its inner secrets.

The genus *Fuchsia* is divided into nine sections, covering the wide range of discovered plant forms. Most are tropical or subtropical shrubs, which vary in height. *F. excorticata* from New Zealand is unusual, in that it is a tree growing up to 12–15m (39–49ft) in its native habitat.

The fuchsias from the section known as *Quelusia* originate from the colder southern parts of South America, and these plants allowed fuchsia cultivars to be developed with winter hardiness. Of these, *F. regia*, *F. magellanica* and *F. coccinea* are the most common and the best varieties for areas with cold winters.

This book lists and describes over 500 fuchsia cultivars – from standards, trained structures and hanging baskets to hardies, Encliandras and unusual cultivars. Each entry describes the flowers and foliage, the growth habit, hardiness, the plant's hybridizer and its year of introduction. At the back of the book, there is a chart showing the colours commonly applied to fuchsia flowers, definitions of the terms used to describe the plant forms, and maps showing the hardiness zones. Every gardener will be able to find something here to inspire them to experiment with some different fuchsia cultivars and planting techniques.

Left: A mixture of hardy fuchsias growing in a border next to a lawn, with dancing red and purple flowers. A fruiting clematis vine with fluffy seed heads can be seen in the background, scrambling over a fence.

Right: A hardy fuchsia growing strongly against a high stone wall, and partially covering a wrought-iron gate.

Standard fuchsias

Please note that standards, even when grown from hardy cultivars, are not frost proof, so treat them as tender subjects, giving them shelter from the frost in the winter. Keeping them ticking over in green leaf is the best way to ensure they survive the winter.

'Alan Titchmarsh'

This has small to medium-sized single or sometimes semi-double flowers. The tube and sepals are rose and the corolla pale lilac-pink. This vigorous, upright cultivar – named after a British celebrity gardener – makes a very nice quarter or half standard. It is a strong grower, covered with flower, but when grown as a pot plant looks untidy in a smaller pot, therefore better grown as a large pot plant. The foliage is mid-green and small to medium-sized. Its introduction was as part of the diamond anniversary celebrations of the British Fuchsia Society. Half hardy; Zones 9–10. Weston, UK, 1998.

'Alf Thornley'

This is well covered in medium-sized double flowers with a pink tube, neyron-rose sepals and a creamy white full corolla, which stand out well against the medium-sized, mid-green foliage. The flowers have a beautiful overall shape and the plant usually produces two at each leaf axil. It is a vigorous, strong growing, upright, self-branching cultivar and makes a terrific half standard. Better grown outside than under glass and enjoys cool shade. Half hardy; Zones 9–10. Clark, UK, 1981.

'Amelie Aubin'

This is an excellent old German cultivar with a strong growing and self-branching, if rather lax habit. It has medium to large single flowers with a long, fat, waxy-white tube, waxy-white horizontal sepals and a rosy-carmine corolla. The foliage is medium to large, mid-green and slightly serrated. It makes an excellent full or half standard, which is slightly weeping, and is good for trained shapes, especially a pyramid. Half hardy; Zones 9–10. Eggbrecht, Germany, 1884.

'Annabel'

This cultivar has medium to large double flowers with a white-striped pink tube, white sepals with pink tips and a full white corolla veined with pink. Growth is upright and self-branching but slightly lax when flowering. It makes a beautiful half standard with its flowers standing out among the large, light-green serrated

'Ballet Girl'

leaves. Also try as a full or quarter standard, in baskets and as a pot plant. Various nurseries call it hardy, but treat with caution. Hardy; Zones 7–8. Ryle, UK, 1977.

'Baby Bright'

The small to medium single flowers have a white tube with a pink blush, white sepals blushed pink and a white corolla blushed pink. The flowers are white when grown in shade but turn pink in sun, and they sit beautifully on the small to medium-sized bright mid-green foliage. It has an upright bushy habit and is excellent grown as a mini or small quarter standard. It also makes an effective small pot plant. Half hardy; Zones 9–10. Bright, UK, 1992.

'Ballet Girl'

This very old but excellent strong-growing bushy cultivar has stood the test of time. The medium to large double flowers have a bright cerise tube and sepals, and a white corolla with red veining. Its strong upright growth habit with attractive mid- to dark green foliage suits training as a half or full standard. Half hardy; Zones 9–10. Veich, UK, 1894.

'Alan Titchmarsh'

'Annabel'

'Barbara'

The flowers of this fuchsia are medium-sized singles with a pale pink tube and sepals, and tangerine-pink corolla. It is a strong, upright grower and the flowers stand out well against the medium-sized light to mid-green foliage. It will make a good quarter or half standard, and grows strongly enough to make a full standard. It tolerates the full sun quite well, so try it as a patio plant or in a summer bedding scheme. It will survive in milder areas planted as a shrub. Frost hardy; Zones 7–8, Tolley, UK, 1971.

'Bicentennial'

This US cultivar has medium-sized double flowers with a white tube flushed orange, orange sepals and a corolla with magenta centre and orange outside petals. Its lax trailing habit makes it effective in a hanging basket or as a weeping standard, but its weeping habit and flower size means it might be best as a half or full standard. The unusual coloured flowers are spectacular among the light to mid-green leaves. Half hardy; Zones 9–10. Paskesen, USA, 1976.

'Caroline'

This is one of a group of fuchsias with very flared, bell-shaped corollas that make a striking sight. The flowers are medium-sized singles with a pink tube, cream-flushed pink sepals and a flared violet corolla. It has strong, upright, self-branching growth

'Celia Smedley'

'Barbara'

with medium-sized mid-green foliage. It makes an excellent eye-catching half standard and grows very well as a pot plant. Half hardy; Zones 9–10. Miller, UK, 1967.

'Celia Smedley'

This cultivar has medium to large single flowers with a neyron-rose tube, neyron-rose sepals and a currant-red corolla. It is very quick growing and vigorous, and becomes a large plant in a single season. It makes a spectacular full standard and a good half standard. If it has a fault, it makes a lot of wood and can be difficult to get back into growth again after pruning back. The large vivid flowers contrast well with the large mid-green leaves. Because of its rapid growth, it also makes a very good specimen patio or container plant. Some growers have success with it as a permanently planted shrub in milder areas. Frost hardy; Zone 8. Bellamy, UK, 1970.

'Checkerboard'

If you have not grown a standard before, this cultivar is an excellent one to choose. It has medium-sized long single flowers with a red tube, red sepals sharply changing to white, and a red corolla

'Checkerboard'

turning white at the base. The flowers stand out and sparkle against the mid-green finely serrated foliage. It makes a very nice full or half standard, and grown in this way it resembles a Christmas tree with all its decorations and lights on. Flowering starts early in the season and it blooms continuously until the autumn. Use this cultivar to try a variety of trained shapes, as it is very adaptable. It is one of those cultivars that should be a part of everyone's collection. Half hardy; Zones 9–10. Walker and Jones, USA, 1948.

'Derby Imp'

This small-flowered cultivar with wiry stems is useful for creating many different trained shapes including standards. The prolific single flowers have a crimson tube and sepals and a violet-blue corolla that is pink at the base of the petals. The small, mid-green foliage complements the flowers very well, and this cultivar can be used as a basket, bush, hanging pot, fan or quarter standard. It only reached the commercial world because of the interest shown by a fuchsia enthusiast, who when visiting Cliff Gadsby's garden took a liking to this seedling among many others that were growing there. Half hardy; Zones 9–10. Gadsby, UK, 1974.

'Doreen Redfern'

'Ernie '

'Doreen Redfern'

The medium-sized single flowers of this fuchsia have a white tube, white sepals tipped green with pale lilac underneath and a violet corolla, maturing to violet-purple, which contrasts well with the small to medium-sized dark green foliage. Grow it as a quarter or half standard, but make sure to grow it in a shady position because it likes cool conditions and dislikes direct sun. It resulted from a cross between 'Cloverdale Pearl' and 'Marin Glow'. Half hardy; Zones 9–10. Redfern, UK, 1984.

'Dusky Beauty'

This has small single flowers with neyron-rose tube and sepals, and pale purple petals with darker picotee edges. This very floriferous fuchsia with mid- to dark green foliage and bushy, self-branching growth is very useful for training as a standard, especially a quarter standard. It makes an attractive pot plant and was used widely as an exhibition cultivar in the 1990s. Half hardy; Zones 9–10. Ryle, UK, 1981.

'Elaine Margaret'

This Australian cultivar has medium to large double flowers with a white tube, long white sepals tinged magenta, and a three-quarter flared white corolla. The buds are long and pointed, with mid-green

foliage. The growth is somewhat lax but it will make a good weeping half or full standard. It is also suitable for baskets and containers. Half hardy; Zones 9–10. Richardson, Australia, 1988.

'Ernie'

This recent cultivar has small to medium-sized single flowers with a red tube, red sepals and a white corolla with red veining. The red colour is rather bright, almost iridescent, and the short corolla has an attractive semi-flared shape. It has

vigorous, upright, self-branching growth with medium to dark green, small narrow leaves, and grows easily as a quarter or half standard. It is also very good as a pot or outdoor container plant. This cultivar is protected by plant breeder's rights. Half hardy; Zones 9–10. Götz, Germany, 2004.

'Ernie Bromley'

This wonderful, adaptable cultivar could be placed in almost any section of this directory. It is hardy with vigorous, slightly lax self-branching growth, and its attractive yellow-green foliage provides the perfect foil to the abundant, intensely coloured flowers. They are medium-sized singles with a pink tube and sepals, and a deep violet, flared corolla. It makes a superb slightly weeping half or full standard, but can also be used for hanging baskets, training as pillars and fans, or as a hardy plant in the border. Hardy; Zone 8. Growth 1m (3ft). Goulding, UK, 1988.

'Evensong'

This is a strong upright that is well suited to growing as a quarter or half standard. It has medium-sized single flowers with a white tube blushed with pink, fully reflexed white sepals with a pink blush at the base, and a white, flared corolla. The growth is quite vigorous and the small to medium-sized foliage is light green. Half hardy; Zones 9–10. Colville, UK, 1967.

'Ernie Bromley'

'Fascination'

This was named 'Emile de Wildeman' when first released but is now commonly known as 'Fascination'. It has very full medium to large double flowers; the tube and sepals are carmine-red and the corolla pink with cerise veining. It is a strong, upright, vigorous grower and can be trained as a superb half or even full standard with its attractive mid-green foliage. It also makes a good pyramid and is happy as a summer bedding plant. This is perhaps one of the best of Lemoine's many introductions. Half hardy; Zones 9–10. Lemoine, France, 1905.

'Flirtation Waltz'

This cultivar from the Waltz stable makes a superb half standard. It has medium double flowers with a creamy white tube, sepals flushed pink and a shell-pink corolla with startling red anthers. The growth is upright and bushy with light to mid-green foliage. It flowers early in the season, but the blooms mark easily when allowed to get wet. Half hardy; Zones 9–10. Waltz, USA, 1962.

'Flying Scotsman'

This is a strong-growing upright with attractive medium-sized double flowers set against the medium-sized mid-green foliage. The flowers have a short white tube with a pink flush turning red on maturity, pink sepals and a full corolla with rosy red petals streaked white. It is easily trained as an excellent half standard and also good as a pot plant or in summer bedding schemes. It is one of a series of cultivars named after famous trains, introduced by Edwin Goulding. Half hardy; Zones 9–10. Goulding, UK, 1985.

'Gay Parasol'

The name describes the flowers of this cultivar very aptly – they open to a rather flat shape, just like a parasol. They are a medium-sized double with an ivory-green tube, pinkish-white sepals and a burgundy-red, flat rosette-shaped corolla. The plant has strong upright growth with mid-green foliage and makes a very nice half standard, or is equally good as a pot

'Flirtation Waltz'

plant. It is one of many excellent introductions by the US hybridist Annabelle Stubbs. Half hardy; Zones 9–10. Stubbs, USA, 1979.

'Grandma Sinton'

This double-flowered cultivar has medium-sized flowers with a pale pink tube striped red, pale pink sepals with green tips

'Gay Parasol'

'Grandma Sinton'

touched red near the base, and a full white to pale pink corolla. It is very free-flowering for a double with rather stiff, wiry lax growth and medium-sized mid-green foliage. Grow it as a slightly weeping half standard or use in hanging baskets, although some weighting might be required to bend down the branches. Half hardy; Zones 9–10. Sinton, UK, 1986.

'Gruss aus dem Bodenthal'

This old German fuchsia (the name means 'Greetings from the Bode Valley') is synonymous with 'Black Prince' and is also known as the 'black fuchsia'. An upright self-branching fuchsia packed with flowers from early to late in the season. Grown as a pot plant it needs very little pinching after the first stop and can easily be grown as a smallish standard; it is not vigorous enough to make a full standard. The small to medium-sized single flowers have a short, rich crimson tube, rich crimson sepals held horizontally and a dark violet-purple corolla, almost black on opening, with small mid-green foliage. Take care when watering it in a pot because it is easy to drown the root system, especially early in the season. Half hardy; Zones 9–10. Sattler and Bethge, Germany, 1893.

'Hampshire Blue'

This strongly upright-growing cultivar with semi-double flowers was a sport from the cultivar 'Carmel Blue'. The flowers are medium in size, semi-double or sometimes single with a cream-flushed pink tube, semi-reflexed cream-flushed pink sepals and a powder blue corolla, with white at the base of the petals. The strong upright growth with medium to large mid-green foliage lends itself to training as a half or full standard. Half hardy; Zones 9–10. Clark, UK, 1983.

'Harbour Bridge'

This double-flowered Australian cultivar is named after the famous Sydney Harbour Bridge. The medium to large double flowers have a short rose tube, rose sepals tipped green and a lavender-blue corolla with pink blotches on the petals. With strong upright growth and mid-green foliage, it is easy to grow as a large standard. Half hardy; Zones 9–10. Lockerbie, Australia, 1971.

'Hazel'

This slightly lax cultivar has large double, rather round flowers with a neyron-rose tube and sepals, and a violet and neyron-rose corolla with purple edges, splashed with white. The flowers contrast well with

'Irene van Zoeren'

the large red-veined, lettuce-green foliage. It is excellent when grown as a weeping full or half standard, used in a hanging basket or as a pot plant with support. Half hardy; Zones 9–10. Richardson, Australia, 1985.

'Ingelore'

This cultivar is quite floriferous and grows well in a sunny position. The small to medium-sized single flowers have a red

tube, horizontal red sepals and a rose-purple corolla with scalloped edges to the petals. The medium-sized ovate leaves are mid-green. Grows well as a quarter or half standard, and is effective in summer bedding schemes or in a pot. Half hardy; Zones 9–10. Strümper, Germany, 1986.

'Irene van Zoeren'

This bushy cultivar has medium double flowers with a light orange tube, rose-red sepals with yellow-green tips and a lilac-rose corolla with a darker red border to the petals. It has a bushy habit with strongly upright growth and makes a nice quarter or half standard, or a good pot plant or specimen plant. It has mid- to dark green foliage and tolerates full sun. Half hardy; Zones 9–10. Beije, Netherlands, 1989.

'Iris Amer'

This compact double cultivar responds well to pinching, forming a tight shape. The medium-sized double flowers have a white tube, white pink-flushed sepals with green tips, and a tight rose-magenta corolla with lighter splashes. The medium-sized foliage is dark green and the growth suits a quarter or half standard. It inherited its free-flowering habit from one of its parents, 'Empress of Prussia'. Half hardy; Zones 9–10. Amer, UK, 1966.

'Hazel'

'Iris Amer'

'Joy Patmore'

'Kolding Perle'

'Jack Acland'

This cultivar has very vigorous stiff trailing growth, with long arched branches and mid-green foliage. It has medium to large single flowers with a medium pink tube, slightly recurving pink sepals and a bell-shaped corolla that opens rose-red and fades to dark pink. It makes a good weeping half or full standard, and is also excellent in a hanging basket. The incorrect spelling of the name as 'Jack Ackland' is often seen and it is also sometimes confused with 'Jack Shaan'. Half hardy; Zones 9–10. Haag and Son, USA, 1952.

'Joan Pacey'

This is an upright, strong-growing cultivar with self-branching growth and mid-green leaves. It flowers over a long period and will happily take full sun. The single flowers are medium-sized with a long white tube blushed pink, pink sepals with green tips and a phlox-pink corolla with red veining. It grows well when trained as a half or full standard, or various trained shapes, including an espalier. Half hardy; Zones 9–10. Gadsby, UK, 1977.

'Joy Patmore'

This striking cultivar has medium-sized single flowers with a white tube, waxy white sepals tipped green and a flared carmine corolla. The colour combination of the flowers is very vivid and they stand out well from the mid-green foliage. It has very strong upright growth and will make an excellent quarter, half or full standard. It will also make a splendid specimen plant, and because of the way it displays its flowers, it will also excel as a summer bedding plant. This cultivar deserves a place in everyone's collection. Half hardy; Zones 9–10. Turner, UK, 1961.

'Katrina Thompsen'

This exhibition-class cultivar bears small to medium single flowers but it compensates for their small size by the sheer number. The flowers have a white-green tube, white sepals and a white corolla. In common with many of the whites, the flower colour will stay white in shade but if exposed to full sun it acquires pink hues. It grows as a vigorous, self-branching and slightly lax bush, excellent as a beautiful quarter standard covered in flowers that stand out against the small, dark green foliage. It is very adaptable and can be trained into various shapes, including a pyramid or column, or simply grown as a pot plant. Beware of fuchsia rust on this cultivar. Half hardy; Zones 9–10. Wilkinson, UK, 1991.

'Kolding Perle'

This is a very vigorous and strong-growing cultivar originating from the Copenhagen area, easy to grow to a large standard in a short space of time. It has quite long inter-nodal joints and is therefore better grown as a full or perhaps a half standard. The medium-sized single flowers have a waxy white tube and sepals, and a pink corolla shaded with cerise and salmon. The flowers are reminiscent of the Lye cultivars, and it is sometimes confused with 'Lye's Unique'. The leaves are large and light to mid-green. Half hardy; Zones 9–10. Unknown raiser, Denmark, unknown release date.

'Kwintet'

This attractive Dutch cultivar has strong upright, bushy growth with medium-sized light to mid-green foliage that is slightly serrated. The attractive medium-sized and almost self-coloured single flowers have a long, dark rose-red tube, reflexed rose-red sepals and a flared rose-red corolla. Very free-flowering, it makes excellent standards, probably best as a half but strong enough for a full standard. Half hardy; Zones 9–10. van Wieringen, Netherlands, 1970.

'Kwintet'

'Love's Reward'

'Margaret Brown'

'Love's Reward'

The name of this cultivar is very apt – the particularly beautiful flowers caused a huge stir among fuchsia growers when it was first released. It has small to medium single flowers that are almost semi-erect and held off the mid-green foliage. The flower has a pink tube, pink sepals and a violet-blue corolla with red stamens. The growth is short, bushy and self-branching, and it makes a very striking quarter standard. You will need to remove any dead foliage quickly, since this cultivar is prone to botrytis in the branches caused by rotting leaves. You should also be sparing with watering, as it hates water-logging. Half hardy; Zones 9–10. Bambridge, UK, 1986.

'Loeky'

This upright self-branching Dutch cultivar (named after the hybridizer's wife) makes an excellent quarter or half standard. The medium-sized single flowers are very distinctive, with the corolla opening flat like a saucer, rather similar to 'Citation'. The tube and sepals are rose-red, the flat corolla is dark mallow-purple, and it has a very long pistil and long, crimson stamens. The leaves are dark green with a serrated edge. Half hardy; Zones 9–10. de Graaff, Netherlands, 1985.

'Lye's Unique'

This is a very old cultivar and perhaps one of the best-known varieties developed by James Lye. The flower is a hanging, medium-sized single with a waxy white tube and sepals (both being a trademark of the Lye varieties) and a salmon-orange corolla. It has upright vigorous growth with mid-green leaves, and flowers early, continuing right through the season. Grows easily and quickly to make an impressive half or full standard. Half hardy; Zones 9–10. Lye, UK, 1886.

'Margaret Brown'

This hardy cultivar is probably one of the best fuchsias there is. It has small single flowers with a rose-pink tube and sepals, and a light rose-bengal corolla with light veining. Its growth is vigorous and upright,

'Lye's Unique'

with light green foliage. It makes a splendid quarter or half standard, or you can grow it as a permanently planted shrub in the garden where it will give years of pleasure with its continuous summer and autumn flowering. It was awarded an RHS Highly Commended Certificate for hardiness in 1965. Hardy; Zone 6. Growth 1m (3ft). Wood, UK, 1939.

'Miss California'

This introduction from the USA has medium to large semi-double flowers with a pink tube, long narrow pink sepals and a flared corolla with white, pink-veined petals. It has reasonably vigorous growth with thin wiry stems and a slightly lax habit. The long flowers show up well against the small to medium and rather narrow mid-green leaves, and it is easy to grow to a quarter or half standard. Half hardy; Zones 9–10. Hodges, USA, 1950.

'Mrs Lovell Swisher'

This is an easy and rewarding fuchsia to grow, recommended for beginners. The small to medium single flowers have a long pink tube, green and pinkish-white sepals held just above the horizontal, and a deep rose corolla. The growth is vigorous and upright with mid-green leaves. The tremendous number of flowers produced over a long season makes up for their smaller size. It is easy to grow to a quarter, half or full standard, although it is probably at its best as a half. Half hardy; Zones 9–10. Evans and Reeves, USA, 1942.

'Nancy Lou'

This has beautiful medium to large double flowers with a pink tube, fully reflexed pink sepals with green tips and a very full, brilliant white corolla. The growth is strongly upright with large mid- to dark green serrated leaves, but it needs some pinching to encourage branching. It is well suited to training as a half or even full standard and makes a striking patio pot plant. Half hardy; Zones 9–10. Stubbs, USA, 1971.

'Nellie Nuttall'

This small, showy cultivar is widely used for exhibitions, and when you see it you can understand why. It has small to medium-sized single flowers that are semi-erect and held out from the mid-green foliage. The tube is small and red, the horizontal sepals crimson and the corolla white with red veining. The growth is upright and very bushy, and it makes a superb edging plant, miniature or quarter standard. The growth is probably not vigorous enough to make a larger standard unless you have a lot of patience and can grow it for a few years. It was hybridized from 'Khada' x 'Icecap'. Half hardy; Zones 9–10. Roe, UK, 1977.

'Norfolk Ivor'

This is a strong-growing upright and self-branching cultivar with mid-green foliage and medium to large, semi-double – sometimes fully double – flowers. The buds are fat and pointed, and the flowers

'Nancy Lou'

have a white tube, white sepals with a hint of pink, and a lavender-blue corolla. It is an excellent cultivar to grow as a larger standard and good as a summer bedding plant. Half hardy; Zones 9–10. Goulding, UK, 1984.

'Olive Smith'

This cultivar has small single flowers held semi-erect from the mid-green foliage, with a carmine tube, carmine sepals that curve upward and a crimson corolla. It has vigorous upright self-branching growth, and the sheer number of flowers produced compensates for their small size. It makes

a superb quarter, half or full standard and is often seen at exhibitions trained this way. It also makes a good summer bedding plant. Half hardy; Zones 9–10. Smith, UK, 1991.

'Orwell'

This is a small, compact fuchsia with mid-green foliage that is excellent as a quarter standard or smaller pot plant. The small to medium double flowers have a short tangerine tube and sepals, and a ruffled, darker tangerine-orange corolla. The colour combination is unusual and striking. Half hardy; Zones 9–10. Goulding, UK, 1987.

'Ortenburger Festival'

This cultivar has very striking flowers that really catch the eye, especially when grown as a standard. It has medium-sized bell-shaped single flowers with a short, thick red tube, deep red sepals held just below the horizontal and a violet-blue corolla turning reddish on maturity. The growth is upright, bushy and self-branching, and the leaves are dark green with serrated edges. A very impressive half or full standard, and older specimens have attractive peeling bark. Half hardy; Zones 9–10. Töpperwein, Germany, 1973.

'Nellie Nuttall'

'Olive Smith'

'Paula Jane'

'Paula Jane'

The medium-sized semi-double flowers of this fuchsia have a pink tube, carmine-rose sepals and a beetroot-purple corolla that matures to ruby red and flares open. The flowers stand out against the shiny light to mid-green foliage. It has strong, upright bushy growth with very sturdy stems, makes an excellent bush and is easy to train as a standard. It is best as a half standard, but can also be grown as a quarter or a full standard. The freely produced pollen tends to be deposited on the leaves, which can look messy, and the firmly attached berries need to be cut off to ensure continued flowering. Half hardy; Zones 9–10. Tite, UK, 1975.

'Rigoletto'

'Peppermint Stick'

This cultivar has a rather unusual flower, as suggested by its name. It has medium-sized double hanging flowers with a carmine-rose tube, carmine sepals with a white stripe and a corolla with purple centre petals and light carmine outer petals with a purple edge. It is very floriferous for the size of the flower, and the growth is strongly upright with mid-green foliage. The two-tone flowers display well when growing it as a half standard. It is also a good choice for a pot or bedding plant. Half hardy; Zones 9–10. Walker and Jones, USA, 1950.

'Perky Pink'

This is a strong upright US cultivar that is bushy and very floriferous with rather narrow, slightly serrated mid-green leaves. The medium-sized double flowers have a short pale pink tube, short broad pink sepals with green tips and a white corolla flushed pale pink and pink veining. It is easy to grow as an excellent half standard. Half hardy; Zones 9–10. Erickson and Lewis, USA, 1959.

'Perry Park'

This British cultivar is a strong-growing and self-branching bush that is excellent as a quarter, half or even full standard. The flower is a medium-sized single with a pale pink tube, pink sepals with green tips and a bright rose corolla, the petals becoming

'Roesse Tethys'

paler at the base. The mid-green foliage is of medium size and the cultivar does well as a pot plant or as a summer bedder in the garden. Half hardy; Zones 9–10. Handley, UK, 1977.

'Rigoletto'

This cultivar has rather unusually shaped flowers, quite freely produced, given their size. They are medium to large doubles with a short, deep red tube and sepals, and a light purple corolla with petals that have frilled edges and are lighter at the base. The whole flower has an attractive triangular shape, which displays beautifully among the light to mid-green foliage. The upright growth is self-branching, making a good half or full standard. Half hardy; Zones 9–10. Blackwell, UK, 1965.

'Roesse Tethys'

This recently introduced cultivar has all the right characteristics for an excellent quarter or half standard. The flowers are quite unusual, being semi-erect small doubles with a vivid red tube and sepals, and a tight burgundy corolla with lighter patches at the base of the petals. The growth is upright, self-branching with light to mid-green foliage, and it is very floriferous for a double, with two or sometimes three flowers per leaf axil. Half hardy; Zones 9–10. Roes, Netherlands, 2004.

'Royal Velvet'

'Shelford'

'Ron Ewart'

This beautiful cultivar, named after a British fuchsia enthusiast and author, is a good upright grower with a self-branching habit. The abundant small single flowers are carried semi-erect and have a white tube and sepals, and a rose-bengal corolla shading to white at the base of the petals. The mid-green foliage is small to medium-sized and a lovely foil for the flower. It excels when grown as any of the smaller sized standards, especially as a quarter standard, and is also good for summer bedding or as a pot plant. Half hardy; Zones 9–10. Roe, UK, 1981.

'Royal Velvet'

This cultivar has medium to large double flowers with a crimson red tube and sepals, and a deep purple corolla splashed with red, which flares very widely open on maturity. The growth is vigorous and upright, with bright light to mid-green foliage. It makes an excellent half or even full standard, but needs pinching well to create branching early in the season. A period grown outside to harden up the growth ensures that the branches are strong enough to support the flowers. It really rewards you when you display the flowers at eye level, but also does well as a summer bedder. This is probably one of Waltz's best introductions, although it has some stiff competition. Half hardy; Zones 9–10. Waltz, USA, 1962.

'Schneeball'

This old German cultivar has an upright and bushy, albeit small, growing habit. The semi-double flowers are medium-sized with a reddish-pink tube, long reddish-pink fully reflexed sepals and a white corolla with pink veining, semi-flared with attractive ruffed petals. The small to medium foliage is light to mid-green. It responds well to standard training and is excellent as a quarter standard. Half hardy; Zones 9–10. Twrdy, Germany, 1874.

'Shelford'

This vigorous and very adaptable cultivar has medium-sized single flowers with a baby pink tube, baby pink sepals shading to white and tipped green, and a white corolla. The amount of pink depends on how much sun it receives; kept in the shade it is almost white. It is vigorous, self-branching and upright and makes an excellent quarter or half standard with very little effort. The flowers stand out well from the medium-sized mid- to dark green foliage. In all ways this is an excellent cultivar, which can be used in baskets and as a summer bedding plant. Half hardy; Zones 9–10. Roe, UK, 1986.

'Sleigh Bells'

This is one of the almost pure white cultivars and has medium-sized single flowers with a white tube, white sepals with green tips and a white corolla. The growth is upright and bushy, with mid- to dark green serrated leaves that contrast beautifully with the flowers. It makes a very good half standard and is excellent trained as a pyramid or espalier. Half hardy; Zones 9–10. Schnabel, USA, 1954.

'Sophie Louise'

This is a compact, attractive and floriferous cultivar introduced by Mel Wilkinson. It has small single flowers with a greenish-white tube, white sepals and a vivid dark purple corolla, which hold themselves semi-erect, contrasting well with the small mid-green foliage. It has a bushy, self-branching habit and grows quite well, but will not make a big plant quickly. Grow as a miniature or quarter standard and it will reward you with a tremendous show of flowers. Half hardy; Zones 9–10. Wilkinson, UK, 1999.

'Sophie Louise'

'Tom Thumb'

Introduced over 150 years ago, this small hardy fuchsia is still very popular, having proved itself reliable and easy to grow. It has small single or semi-double flowers with a carmine tube and sepals, and a mauve-carmine veined corolla. The flowers hang down among the small, dark green leaves. It has compact, upright bushy growth and makes a superb miniature or quarter standard. It is equally at home in the rockery or for edging borders. It was awarded an RHS First Class Certificate for hardiness in 1962. Hardy; Zone 6. Growth 46cm (18in). Baudinat, France, 1850.

'Torvill and Dean'

This is a strong, upright growing cultivar named after the famous British ice-dancing couple. It has large double flowers with a pale cerise tube, pale cerise sepals tipped green and a full white corolla flushed cerise with pale cerise veining. The attractive dark green foliage is a perfect foil for the flowers, which stand out beautifully. It makes an impressive sight when trained as a half or full standard, but you need to ensure that the trunk and stems have developed hard wood, otherwise the weight of the flowers can cause branches to break in strong wind and rain. Half hardy; Zones 9–10. Pacey, UK, 1985.

'Tom Thumb'

'Tsjiep'

This Dutch fuchsia, hybridized by Herman de Graaff and named after his son, is a delightful floriferous cultivar for training as a small standard, excelling as a miniature or quarter standard. The small single flowers have a longish cream tube, cream sepals blushed rose and a blood-red corolla maturing to claret. It has attractive light to mid-green foliage, while the growth is upright and bushy. Half hardy; Zones 9–10. de Graaff, Netherlands, 1981.

'Ullswater'

'Ullswater'

With its bushy and upright growth, this makes a good half standard. It has medium to large double flowers with a long pale pink tube, long pale pink sepals and a compact orchid-blue corolla fading to orchid-purple. The medium to large leaves are mid-green, and contrast well against the attractive pastel-coloured flowers. Half hardy; Zones 9–10. Travis, UK, 1958.

'Vanessa Jackson'

This cultivar has long, large single flowers with a salmon-red tube, long salmon-orange sepals and a trumpet-shaped salmon-orange and red corolla. The trailing, self-branching growth, with large mid-green leaves, makes a lovely weeping standard, and it is also ideal for hanging baskets and pots. Half hardy; Zones 9–10. Handley, UK, 1980.

'Vivian Harris'

This strong upright and bushy fuchsia with light to mid-green foliage is easy to train as a standard, excelling as a half standard. It resulted from a cross between 'Rufus' and 'Leverhulme', and inherited characteristics from both parents. The medium-sized Triphylla-type flowers have a long turkey-red tube, short turkey-red sepals and a deeper turkey-red corolla. Half hardy; Zones 9–10. Harris, UK, 1977.

'Torvill and Dean'

'Waltzing Matilda'

Named after the famous Australian folk song, this cultivar grows as a lax bush with light green, red-veined foliage. The flower buds are large and pointed, and the large double flowers have a pale pink tube, sepals that are light pink on top but darker underneath and a full, pale pink corolla with the outer petals streaked with rose. It is easy to train as a semi-weeping standard – the taller the better because of the flower size – and excellent for use in a container. Half hardy; Zones 9–10. Bromat, Australia, 1989.

'WALZ Kalebas'

This is an easily grown, bushy, multi-flowering cultivar with dull green foliage. The medium-sized single flowers have an unusual rose-red, rather pear-shaped tube, rose-red sepals with yellow-green tips curved upwards and a mid-red corolla. It is easy to grow as a quarter or half standard, and the unusual shape of the flowers makes it rather striking. Half hardy; Zones 9–10. Waldenmaier, Netherlands, 1990.

'Wigan Peer'

This is a relative newcomer, with small to medium-sized compact double flowers with a pink tube, white sepals flushed pale pink and a full white corolla. It is a strong

'WALZ Kalebas'

upright, self-branching fuchsia with mid-green foliage, and makes a good quarter or half standard. It is also an excellent pot plant because of the abundant, long-lasting flowers. Half hardy; Zones 9–10. Clark, UK, 1988.

'Winston Churchill'

This lovely free-flowering double-flowered cultivar has medium-sized compact blooms with a pink tube and sepals, and a lavender-blue corolla with reddish veins. It has upright and bushy self-branching

'Winston Churchill'

growth with wiry stems and rather narrow small mid- to dark green foliage. It makes a very nice quarter or half standard, and also makes a good pot plant. It is a good, reliable cultivar. Half hardy; Zones 9–10. Garson, USA, 1942.

'Yvonne Holmes'

This cultivar has a bushy upright habit and is very free-flowering, with light to mid-green foliage, and newer growth a very light shade of green. The flower is a medium-sized single with a crimson tube, crimson sepals tipped green and a cyclamen-purple bell-shaped corolla, carmine at the base of the petals. It is easy to grow as an excellent quarter or half standard, and might be worth trying as a hardy, since it has a hardy cultivar in its parentage. Half hardy; Zones 9–10. Holmes, UK, 1974.

'Zaanlander'

This vigorous cultivar has strong upright growth and mid-green foliage, and is easy to train as a standard. The medium-sized single flowers have a longish pink tube flushed white, narrow orchid-pink sepals and a violet-purple corolla with white patches at the base of the petals. The abundant flowers mean it also looks good in a patio container but better in a shaded or part shaded location. Half hardy; Zones 9–10. Krom, Netherlands, 1989.

'Wigan Peer'

Trained structures

Fuchsia structures such as pyramids and fans are a challenge to grow but very satisfying when they are complete. It is best to overwinter them in green leaf with minimal heat to ensure that all parts of the structure will start to grow evenly again in the spring.

'Amy Lye'
This fuchsia is a cultivar bred by James Lye, who was one of the earliest producers to grow fuchsia pyramids. It is free- and early-flowering, with medium-sized single flowers that have a creamy white tube, white sepals tipped green and a coral-orange corolla. The growth is vigorous and spreading with medium-sized dark green leaves and is good for training as any tall structure such as a pillar or pyramid. Half hardy; Zones 9–10. Lye, UK, 1885.

'Beacon Rosa'
A sport from 'Beacon', this fuchsia inherits the same growth and similar darkish green leaves with wavy serrated edges, but with different flowers. They are medium-sized single flowers with a pink tube, pink sepals and a flared pink corolla with red veining on the petals. This cultivar is excellent for training as a fan, pyramid or standard,

'Beacon Rosa'

'Brutus'

and is a good garden hardy. Branches can occasionally partially revert to the darker flower colours of the parent; you need to cut these out at the point of origin or they will gradually take over the whole plant. Hardy; Zones 6–7. Growth 60cm (2ft). Bürgi and Ott, Switzerland, 1972.

'Berkeley'
Named after the city of Berkeley in California, this has large double flowers with a red-striped pale rose tube, large pale rose recurved sepals and a violet-pink corolla with salmon-pink at the base of the petals. The growth is vigorously upright but slightly lax, with mid- to dark green foliage. It is very floriferous for a large double, and is suitable to grow as a pyramid or similar trained shape. Half hardy; Zones 9–10. Reiter, USA, 1955.

'Brutus'
This is a vigorous hardy cultivar, which is very floriferous and bushy. It has wiry, arching growth with medium-sized mid-green foliage. The flowers are single but can often contain extra petaloids, making them into a semi-double; they have a rich cerise tube and sepals and a dark purple corolla. The manner of growth allows training to almost any shape, but this

'Ellen Morgan'

plant excels when trained as a pyramid, looking like a Christmas tree with lots of sparkling decorations. It is an adaptable cultivar, also trainable as a pillar, espalier or standard. Hardy; Zones 6–7. Growth 65cm (26in). Bull, UK, 1901.

'Crosby Soroptimist'
The medium-sized single flowers of this fuchsia have a short pink tube, long reflexed pink sepals and a short, white corolla with burgundy anthers and stigma. The pure colours of the flowers beautifully complement the medium-sized dark green foliage and the growth is upright, bushy and slightly wiry. It is excellent for growing upright, trained shapes and easy to grow as a bush or standard. Half hardy; Zones 9–10. Clark, UK, 1989.

'Ellen Morgan'
This seedling from 'Phyllis' has good upright self-branching growth that is excellent for growing trained shapes, standards and even to use as a bedding plant. The medium-sized double flowers have a short, thin white tube with green stripes, white sepals with green tips and a flaring mallow-purple corolla, with rose at the petal base and rose veining. Half hardy; Zones 9–10. Holmes, UK, 1976.

'Fuchsiade '88'

Named after a Dutch fuchsia festival, this has upright self-branching growth, small dark green leaves and an abundance of small single flowers with a reddish-purple tube, reddish-purple sepals that are lighter underneath and a dark purple quarter-flared corolla. It is very adaptable and easily trained into various smaller-scale shapes. Half hardy; Zones 9–10. de Graaff, Netherlands, 1989.

'Harlow Carr'

This is a very floriferous cultivar, suitable for growing smaller-scale trained shapes. It has slightly lax, upright, self-branching bushy growth with small, dark green leaves against which the flowers make a good contrast. The flowers are medium-sized singles with a pale pink tube, medium-length, recurving pink sepals and a white corolla with red anthers. It grows very easily to make an attractive small to medium-sized pyramid or pillar, and is also worth trying as a small fan. Half hardy; Zones 9–10. Johns, UK, 1991.

'James Lye'

This old British cultivar, named after the grower himself, has perfectly shaped medium-sized double flowers with a cerise tube, cerise sepals held horizontally and a bluish-mauve corolla that is pale mauve at

'Harlow Carr'

the base of the petals. The growth is strongly upright with medium-sized mid-green foliage, and it is easily trained into tall shapes such as pyramids, pillars and standards. It is sometimes confused with 'Constance', another of Lye's cultivars. Half hardy; Zones 9–10. Lye, UK, 1883.

'Lillian Annetts'

This fuchsia quickly became very popular after its introduction because of its beautiful flowers and tremendous versatility. The flower is a small to medium double with a white tube striped green,

white sepals and a lavender-blue corolla with patches of white and pink at the base of the petals. The upright lax growth is short-jointed and bushy, with small to medium mid-green foliage. This cultivar can be grown to most shapes, but it really excels as a fan. It is very floriferous and continues to flower over a long period. Half hardy; Zones 9–10. Clark, UK, 1993.

'Lindisfarne'

Named after the tidal island off the coast of Northumberland in the UK, this has small, semi-double flowers with a short, thick, pale pink tube, pale pink sepals held horizontally and a deep violet-blue corolla that holds its colour well. The growth is upright, short-jointed and self-branching, with small to medium-sized bright mid-green foliage. It is terrific for most types of trained shapes, excelling as a pyramid, pillar or standard. Half hardy; Zones 9–10. Ryle and Atkinson, UK, 1974.

'Little Beauty'

This is aptly named, with its small to medium-sized single flowers sparking among the small, dark green foliage. The flower has a pinkish-red tube and sepals and the corolla is lavender-blue. The wiry, slightly brittle growth makes a good pyramid or pillar. Half hardy; Zones 9–10. Raiser and date unknown.

'Lillian Annetts'

'Little Beauty'

'Marin Glow'

'Marin Glow'

This impressive fuchsia has medium-sized single flowers with a short white tube, white sepals with green tips and an imperial-purple corolla fading to magenta. The striking flowers seem to glow, standing out from the medium-sized mid-green serrated leaves. This cultivar is free-flowering, with upright and self-branching growth, and makes a very good pyramid or pillar, or a half or full standard. It is better to grow it in partial shade, as the sun will cause the corolla colour to fade. Half hardy; Zones 9–10. Reedstrom, USA, 1954.

'Melody'

This free-flowering US cultivar is an easy grower and has strong, upright bushy growth with attractive, bright green foliage. The medium-sized single flowers have a pale rose-pink tube, pale rose-pink reflexed sepals and a pale cyclamen-purple corolla. It excels when grown as a trained shape and makes a very good standard. Half hardy; Zones 9–10. Reiter, USA, 1942.

'Midwinter'

This is a smaller-growing cultivar which can be used for small pyramids, fans or standards. It has small to medium single flowers with a white tube veined with pink and white sepals, and a white corolla, inspiring its name. The growth is upright, slightly lax and self-branching, with dull, dark green foliage. Take care with the watering of this cultivar as it despises being overwatered. Half hardy; Zones 9–10. Flemming, UK, 1990.

'Mrs Marshall'

This very old cultivar is still widely grown today. It has medium-sized single flowers with a waxy cream-white tube and sepals, and a rose-cerise corolla. The growth is vigorous and upright with medium-sized mid-green foliage. It makes a very nice pyramid-trained plant, and is also good as a standard. When first introduced,

'Midwinter'

it was named 'Grand Duchess Marie'. Half hardy; Zones 9–10. Jones, UK, probably introduced in 1862.

'Phyllis'

This strong-growing upright cultivar has an abundance of small semi-double flowers with a waxy rose tube and sepals, and a rosy cerise corolla. It has a tendency to produce flowers with more than four sepals. The growth is very vigorous with shiny mid-green foliage, and it is easily trained to excellent large pyramids and standards. It is a superb variety to use as a hedge up to 1–1.3m (3–4ft) high because of its hardy nature and growth habit. It was introduced by H.A. Brown, but according to Leo Boullemier the seedling's origin was from continental Europe. Hardy; Zone 6. Brown, UK, 1938.

'President George Bartlett'

Named after a former president of the British Fuchsia Society, this has small to medium-sized semi-double flowers with a burgundy-red tube and sepals, and a dark aubergine corolla, fading with age. The growth is upright and vigorous with a slightly lax habit, and the foliage is a glossy dark green. It is a very adaptable fuchsia – training to virtually any shape is possible, but it is particularly good as a fan, pyramid or standard. It is also very suitable for growing in hanging baskets or pots. Half hardy; Zones 9–10. Bielby and Oxtoby, UK, 1997.

'Phyllis'

'Sir Alfred Ramsey'

This fuchsia is named after England's World Cup winning football team manager, who was also a past president of the East Anglian Fuchsia Fellowship. It has large single flowers with a rose tube, neyron-rose sepals with recurved tips and a quarter-flared corolla that opens violet-purple and matures to violet-red. It has strong, upright self-branching growth with large, attractive light green leaves, and is good for all tall-trained forms, most especially pyramids and standards. Half hardy; Zones 9–10. Goulding, UK, 1984.

'Snowcap'

This is a very easy cultivar to grow, strongly recommended to anyone new to growing fuchsias, as well as those wanting to train an upright shape for the first time. The flowers are medium-sized semi-doubles with a bright red tube and sepals and a white-veined red fluffy corolla. The growth is vigorous, upright and self-branching, with small to medium dark green foliage, and it is very floriferous, with the flowers standing out well from a distance. It can be trained into most upright forms – pillar, pyramid, conical or espalier – and is also very good as a standard or a permanent planting. It works well as a quarter, half or full standard, but best as a half or full. Since it is not at all lax, it does not work well as a fan or in a hanging basket. Hardy; Zones 7–8. Growth 60cm (2ft). Henderson, UK, 1888.

'WALZ Bella'

'Suikerbossie' ('Sugarbush')

This cultivar has upright, self-branching growth. Left to its own devices it will form a natural conical shape, making it a good choice for training into small pyramids, conicals and pillars. It is extremely floriferous with small single flowers with a light green tube flushed pink, empire-rose sepals with green tips and a lilac-violet corolla. The large number of flowers sometimes hides the small, dark olive-green leaves, which are lighter underneath. Half hardy; Zones 9–10. Brouwer, Netherlands, 1985.

'Vivienne Thompson'

This attractive cultivar has medium, upright, self-branching growth with small light to mid-green foliage, and

'Waveney Gem'

is an excellent choice for training any of the upright shapes. The flowers are medium-sized semi-doubles with a pink tube, half-reflexed pink sepals with a neyron rose edge and green tips, and a white corolla veined with neyron-rose. It flowers over a long period and is best in partial shade. Half hardy; Zones 9–10. Reynolds, UK, 1983.

'WALZ Bella'

This strong-growing Dutch cultivar has large, ovate leaves in mid-green with serrated edges and magenta stems. The medium-sized single flowers have a long, thick orange tube, mandarin-orange sepals held downwards and a scarlet corolla, which matures to orange-rose. Its upright growth habit lends it to training into tall, upright shapes, especially standards and pillars. Half hardy; Zones 9–10. Waldenmaier, Netherlands, 1987.

'Waveney Gem'

This cultivar is strong-growing, self-branching and slightly lax with small mid-green leaves. It is very versatile and can be used in baskets or trained as pyramids, conicals, pillars, fans and standards. It excels when trained into a fan shape. The small to medium single flowers have a white tube and sepals, and a mauve corolla. This free-flowering fuchsia is quite quick to come into flower after a final pinch and is well worth a place in any collection. Half hardy; Zones 9–10. Burns, UK, 1985.

'Snowcap'

Hanging baskets and pots

Fuchsias commercially sold as basket cultivars have growth that is lax, trailing or cascading. Those with lax growth tend to have large double flowers, with the weight of the flowers bending down the branches; these types are particularly spectacular.

'Ada Perry'
This is one of many wonderful large, double-flowered trailing cultivars hybridized by the Americans – Annabelle Stubbs being one of the greatest exponents of this art. This cultivar has a rather stiff habit, with large dark green leaves that are distinctively red-veined. The large double flowers have a scarlet tube and sepals with a darker shade underneath and a full blue-purple corolla, streaked with rose. It is ideal for hanging baskets but also makes a splendid weeping half or full standard. It is rather tender and needs a heated greenhouse over the winter to stay at its best. Frost tender; Zone 11. Stubbs, USA, 1983.

'Allure'
This Dutch introduction has large double flowers with a very long, thin, ivory-white tube, white sepals flushed pink, which are semi-recurving, and a full pink corolla.

'Auntie Jinks'

'Allure'

The foliage is mid-green and the growth quite vigorous. This cultivar does not flourish in full sun, faring better when grown in semi-shade. Half hardy; Zones 9–10. Moerman, Netherlands, 1991.

'Annabelle Stubbs'
Named after the famous US hybridizer, this cultivar certainly should be special. The flowers are large full doubles with a light pink tube, coral-pink sepals and a reddish-purple corolla. The foliage is large and mid-green, and the fuchsia is excellent in hanging baskets where the large double flowers are an impressive sight. Half hardy; Zones 9–10. Riley, USA, 1991.

'Auntie Jinks'
This trailing fuchsia should be in every collection because it is so adaptable and can be used in a variety of garden sites. The medium-sized single flowers have a pink-red tube with stripes, white sepals and a cerise-purple corolla with paler patches at the base of the petals. The colour of the corolla fades as the flower matures. It is extremely floriferous, with the pointed buds looking very attractive against the small mid-green foliage. Use it in hanging baskets, hanging pots or to trail over the edge of a container. It also makes

a small weeping standard and can be used for other smaller trained shapes. Half hardy; Zones 9–10. Wilson, UK, 1970.

'Baby Pink'
This very pretty fuchsia from the USA has lovely trailing growth ideally suited to hanging baskets. The dark green leaves have a red central vein, green veins and red stems. It is surprisingly floriferous considering the size of the flowers, which are medium to large doubles, and are almost Triphylla-like, with a long white tube tinged green. The sepals are light pink with green tips that cup the corolla, first curving down and then up; the corolla is very full and tight, pale pink with dark pink veins. Half hardy; Zones 9–10. Soo Yun, USA, 1976.

'Blowick'
This cultivar is an adaptable plant that you can train to almost any shape, and makes an excellent basket. It has the growth habit of a lax bush with mid-green foliage and very pretty medium-sized single flowers. The flowers have a flesh pink tube and sepals and a mallow-purple corolla fading to an attractive shade of plum with age. This cultivar is also easy to train as a standard, with perhaps a half standard being the best. Half hardy; Zones 9–10. Porter, UK, 1984.

'Baby Pink'

'Blush of Dawn'

'Blue Butterfly'

This is excellent for hanging baskets because of its lax growth covered in dark green foliage. The medium to large semi-double flowers have a short white tube, broad white sepals and a deep violet-blue corolla splashed white that opens on maturity to reveal the lighter blue inner petals. Half hardy; Zones 9–10. Waltz, USA, 1960.

'Blush of Dawn'

This exceptional cultivar is not a true trailer but has the growth habit of a lax bush, with mid-green foliage and the weight of the large double flowers bending the branches down. The flowers appear quite late in the season but are worth waiting for. They have a waxy white tube, reflexed waxy white sepals tipped green and a full corolla in an unusual silver-grey and lavender-blue. It is excellent grown in hanging baskets, half baskets or as a half standard. Half hardy; Zones 9–10. Martin, USA, 1962.

'Caradella'

This cultivar has a striking flower that really catches the eye against the trailing mid- to dark green foliage. The medium single flowers have a pink tube and sepals and a violet-pink corolla. It is extremely free-flowering. While it is well worth growing in all sorts of hanging containers, it really excels in hanging pots. Half hardy; Zones 9–10. Delaney, UK, 1992.

'Cascade'

This cultivar is true to its name, with long cascading growths bearing many flowers at the ends. The flower is a medium single with a thin white tube flushed carmine, thin white sepals flushed carmine, which are

'Claudia'

held at the horizontal, and a deep carmine corolla. The foliage is medium to large mid-green and serrated. It is a very good cultivar for mixed baskets and can also be grown on its own, although it tends not to flower much on the top of the basket. Half hardy; Zones 9–10. Lagen, USA, 1937.

'Cecile'

This is a very large double-flowering cultivar which has plenty of flowers for its flower size. The flowers have a pink tube, broad deep pink-red sepals and a lavender-blue corolla that is very full and frilled. The foliage is light mid-green, and the flowers and fat pointed buds stand out from this beautifully. This is a deservedly popular cultivar and well worth growing on its own or in a mixed basket. Half hardy; Zones 9–10. Whitfield, USA, 1981.

'Claudia'

This newish trailing cultivar, with light to mid-green foliage and vigorous self-branching growth, is good for hanging baskets and mixed containers. It is very floriferous over a long period, with medium-sized double flowers with a light rose tube and sepals, and an orchid-pink corolla. Half hardy; Zones 9–10. Sinton, UK, 2000.

'Cecile'

'Dancing Flame'

This cultivar has a rather unusual and distinctive flower colouring. The flowers are often smaller and semi-double at first, but after a short period of flowering, they change to a medium-sized double. The tube is pale orange with darker stripes, the sepals are orange and darker underneath, and the corolla is orange-carmine, with the petal colour darker in the centre. It has stiff trailing growth with rather large mid- to dark green leaves, which set off the flower colour well. This fuchsia is ideal for use in mixed baskets. Half hardy; Zones 9–10. Stubbs, USA, 1981.

'Dee Star'

This Australian cultivar is a natural trailer with mid-green foliage and an added advantage of a long flowering season. The flower is a large double with a medium to long greenish-white tube that takes on a pink flush with more exposure to the sun, long rose-white sepals and a violet corolla maturing to reddish-violet-purple. It is an excellent cultivar to use in hanging baskets and mixed containers. Half hardy; Zones 9–10. Richardson, Australia, 1986.

'Deep Purple'

'Dancing Flame'

'Deep Purple'

This is a large-flowered basket cultivar from the USA with a spreading, trailing habit and medium-sized mid-green foliage. The large double flower has a medium-length white tube, white recurving sepals and a very full, dark purple corolla, which matures to purple on aging. It has a lovely colour contrast between the sepals, corolla and the leaf colour. It is excellent for use in a baskets or hanging containers, and with care can be grown to a weeping standard. Half hardy; Zones 9–10. Garrett, USA, 1989.

'Devonshire Dumpling'

This aptly named fuchsia freely produces large, fat double flowers that are superb in a hanging basket. Each flower emerges from a large, fat, slightly pointed bud and has a medium-length white tube and broad neyron-rose sepals that reflex strongly when the flower is fully open. The corolla is large and fluffy, with the outer white petals flushed pink and the inner petals white. The foliage is medium-sized and mid-green and although the growth is quite stiff, the huge quantities of large

blooms cause the branches to bend down. The flowering period is surprisingly long for such a large flower. Half hardy; Zones 9–10. Hilton, UK, 1981.

'Ebbtide'

This unusual cultivar has vigorous, cascading growth, mid-green foliage and red wiry stems. It is an early-flowering cultivar, and the large white pointed buds open to reveal a large double flower, the tube changing from white to deep pink just before the flower opens. The sepals are white on top and pink beneath, and the light blue and pink corolla opens very wide and matures to lavender-pink. Half hardy; Zones 9–10. Erickson and Lewis, USA, 1959.

'Emma Louise'

This cultivar is superb in a hanging pot, producing abundant, flower-covered growth. The small to medium-sized double flowers have a pink tube and sepals and a powder blue and pale pink full corolla. The foliage is small and mid-green, and the growth is trailing and self-branching. It is also very good for mixed baskets and containers. Half hardy; Zones 9–10. Horsham, UK, 1990.

'Emma Louise'

'Eusebia'

'Eureka Red'

This beautiful fuchsia is ideal for mixed hanging baskets and containers. It has large double flowers with a lovely two-tone colour. They have a greenish-white tube, deep rose sepals and a red or red-purple corolla that flares fully when mature. The medium to large foliage is dark green and the growth quite vigorous. Half hardy; Zones 9–10. Stubbs, USA, 1991.

'Eusebia'

This is a beautiful double-flowering cultivar from Annabelle Stubbs, named after one of her sisters. With rather stiff trailing or semi-trailing vigorous growth and plenty of medium to large double flowers, it is terrific in hanging baskets. The flowers have a greenish-white tube, white sepals with carmine splashes and a carmine-red corolla with white streaks on the petals. The foliage is an attractive mid-green. It makes an elegant weeping standard. Half hardy; Zones 9–10. Stubbs, USA, 1982.

'Falling Stars'

The classically shaped flowers of this fuchsia cascade off the trailing growth with its large mid-green leaves. The medium-sized single flowers have a pinkish-red tube, reddish-pink sepals

'Falling Stars'

and red corolla. It makes a superb half basket but also grows well in hanging baskets and pots. It can also be trained as a weeping half or full standard. Pinch it out well early on, because it is not a naturally self-branching cultivar. Half hardy; Zones 9–10. Reiter, USA, 1941.

'Fey'

This Australian cultivar has lax but stiff, trailing growth and light to mid-green foliage. It is excellent for hanging baskets, containers or as a weeping standard. The flowers are medium to large doubles with a white tube, slightly twisted white sepals and a full lilac corolla with the petals held tightly together, contrasting nicely with the foliage. Half hardy; Zones 9–10. Lockerbie, Australia, 1970.

'Frank Unsworth'

This is an excellent cultivar in hanging pots, small hanging baskets and mixed containers. It has short-jointed vigorous growth with a lax self-branching habit and small dark green leaves. The double flowers are small to medium-sized with a full white tube, white sepals with green tips and a white corolla with a hint of pink at the petal base. The flowers stay white even in sun, but gradually take on extra hints of pink. Half hardy; Zones 9–10. Clark, UK, 1982.

'Frosted Flame'

This cultivar is a natural trailer that makes a superb full or half basket. The medium-sized single flowers have a white tube and sepals, and a distinctive barrel-shaped flame-red corolla. The petals have a darker edge and are lighter towards the base. The medium-sized foliage is bright green and the growth strong. Pinch it well early on to get the best shape. Half hardy; Zones 9–10. Hanley, UK, 1975.

'Frosted Flame'

'Gerharda's Aubergine'

'Golden Marinka'

'Greg Walker'

This Australian cultivar has lax spreading growth and is beautiful in a hanging basket, but you can also grow it as a pot plant supported by canes. The medium-sized double flowers have a white tube striped with carmine-rose, white-carmine sepals and a full violet corolla with red splashes. The new foliage is light green but matures to mid-green later in the season. Half hardy; Zones 9–10. Richardson, Australia, 1982.

'Harry Grey'

This fuchsia should be in everyone's collection, and is very adaptable in use. The small double flowers have a rose pink-streaked tube, white sepals and a fluffy white corolla, but the colours will become pale pink in the sun. The foliage is small, dark green and very dense on the vigorous self-branching wiry growth. It produces flowers as freely as a single-flowered cultivar, often starting to flower eight to nine weeks after the final pinching. It is suitable for all sorts of hanging containers, either planted in groups together or mixed with other plants. It will also make a good mini or quarter standard, or other smaller trained shapes. Half hardy; Zones 9–10. Dunnett, UK, 1980.

'Gerharda's Aubergine'

This stiff trailing cultivar introduced from the Netherlands has small to medium-sized single flowers. The tube and sepals are aubergine and the corolla is an aubergine colour that is very dark on opening, maturing to beetroot-red. It is a vigorous cultivar with mid- to dark green leaves that makes an excellent hanging basket or hanging pot. The colours are well set off by growing it with white or light pink fuchsias. Half hardy; Zones 9–10. de Graaff, Netherlands, 1989.

'Gloria Johnson'

This unusual trailing cultivar has very large flowers, 10cm (4in) long, which are extremely eye-catching. The single flowers have a long pink tube, long thin pale pink sepals held out below the horizontal and a bright rose corolla. The foliage is mid-green and the growth is strong with a vigorous trailing habit. If you want to try something different in a basket that looks a bit out of the ordinary look no further. This cultivar will turn heads. Half hardy; Zones 9–10. Bielby and Oxtoby, UK, 1994.

'Golden Anniversary'

This is a superb and very popular cultivar from Annabelle Stubbs that is good for hanging baskets, but you can also use it in other containers, both on its own and with other plants, and as a weeping standard. The flowers are medium to large full doubles with a greenish-white tube, broad white sepals and a dark violet corolla that fades to rich ruby. The medium to large foliage is light golden-green and provides a beautiful foil to the flowers. Half hardy; Zones 9–10. Stubbs, USA, 1980.

'Golden Marinka'

This is a sport from the famous basket cultivar 'Marinka', and probably one of the best trailing fuchsias with variegated foliage. The medium-sized single flowers are similar to the parent, with the tube, sepals and corolla being similar shades of red, contrasting well with the yellow, green and red foliage. Growth is not quite as vigorous as 'Marinka', but it is excellent for baskets and mixed containers. The best foliage colours develop with good exposure to the sun. Half hardy; Zones 9–10. Weber, USA, 1955.

'Harry Grey'

'Haute Cuisine'

'Holly's Beauty'

'Haute Cuisine'

This wonderful Dutch cultivar is worth planting for its flowers and foliage, even though the growth is a bit untidy. The flowers are medium to large doubles with a dark red tube and sepals, and a wonderful dark aubergine corolla with red anthers and pistil. They make a striking contrast against the medium to large pale to mid-green foliage. The best description of the growth is strong, spreading and lax. It is good for mixed baskets and containers, and makes a lovely weeping standard. Half hardy; Zones 9–10. de Graaff, Netherlands, 1988.

'Hermiena'

This is an excellent, floriferous, self-branching cultivar that is ideal for hanging pots, small hanging baskets and mixed containers. The single flowers are small to medium-sized with both the tube and sepals in white with a hint of pink, and the corolla opening dark violet and maturing to dark plum, nicely contrasting with the small mid-green foliage. It does best with some shade and dislikes being over-watered. Half hardy; Zones 9–10. van Lavieren, Netherlands, 1987.

'Holly's Beauty'

This has large double flowers with a white tube, white sepals flushed pale rose and a pale lavender-lilac full corolla, an extremely pretty, unusual colour. The growth is trailing, with light to mid-green foliage, and it is very attractive in hanging baskets and containers. The colour looks superb blended with other blues and whites in a mixed basket. It resulted from a cross between 'Quasar' and 'Applause', and when first released it was subject to a trademark in California. Half hardy; Zones 9–10. Garrett, USA, 1989.

'Imperial Fantasy'

This is a very impressive and striking US cultivar, with trailing growth suitable for hanging baskets or containers. The large double flowers have a greenish-white tube, white sepals with a hint of red at the base and a full purple corolla with the outer petals splashed with white and pink patches. The leaves are large and dark green with distinctive red veins. Half hardy; Zones 9–10. Stubbs, USA, 1981.

'Intercity'

This trailing cultivar has medium-sized single flowers with a white tube, white sepals flushed pink with green tips and a lilac corolla with scalloped edges to the petals. The flowers are a nice contrast with the mid-green foliage, and this fuchsia is easy to grow in hanging baskets and does well in mixed containers. Half hardy; Zones 9–10. Strümper, Germany, 1986.

'Irene Sinton'

This cultivar, named after the hybridizer's sister-in-law, has large double flowers with a blush-pink tube and sepals, and a pale lilac corolla splashed pink with red veining on the petals. It has semi-lax growth with small to medium-sized mid-green leaves. It grows well in hanging baskets and hanging pots. It is prone to botrytis, so guard against stagnant, humid air around it, and do not overwater, especially in the early stages. Half hardy; Zones 9–10. Sinton, UK, 2004.

'Irene Sinton'

'Jack Shahan'

'Jess'

'Jack Shahan'

This rather stiff trailing fuchsia is one that has maintained its popularity over a number of years. It is very good for baskets, half baskets and even as a weeping standard. The flower is almost a self-coloured medium to large single with quite a long pale rose-bengal tube and rose-bengal sepals and corolla. The narrow leaves are mid-green and serrated. The growth can be a little wild, but it flowers continuously over a long period. Half hardy; Zones 9–10. Tiret, USA, 1949.

'Jane Humber'

The weight of the flowers of this cultivar causes the stems to bend down enough to overcome its stiff growth habit, making it effective in a hanging basket or container. The large double flowers have a pink tube, with broad pink sepals held slightly above the horizontal and a full rose-purple corolla with slightly darker petal edges. The foliage is mid-green while the very round fat buds are pink, adding to the attraction. Half hardy; Zones 9–10. Bielby, UK, 1983.

'Janice Ann'

This is a rather lax self-branching plant, which does well in hanging containers and makes a very nice hanging pot. The single flowers are small to medium with a turkey-red tube and sepals and a violet-blue corolla with bright pink anthers and pistil. The flowers stand out well on the dark green foliage and often appear to sparkle,

particularly if the container is in a shady position, catching the ambient light. It makes an excellent standard and is worth growing as trained shapes, especially as a fan or a small pyramid. Half hardy; Zones 9–10. Holmes, UK, 1994.

'Jess'

Vigorous and lax, this fuchsia is very floriferous and is ideal in hanging baskets or hanging pots. The flowers are medium-sized singles with a long, quite thin rose tube, broad deep rose sepals and a vivid cerise corolla. The medium-sized leaves are mid-green and shiny, and the fat round flower buds add an extra attraction to the display. Half hardy; Zones 9–10. Meier, UK, 1987.

'Jimmy Carr'

This double cultivar has a good cascading habit, making it suitable for all kinds of hanging containers. The flowers are medium-sized doubles with a white-striped pink tube, horizontal white sepals with a hint of pink and a full purple corolla maturing to magenta, with light splashes at the base of the petals. It is quite free-flowering, and the flower colours contrast well with the medium-sized mid-green foliage. Half hardy; Zones 9–10. Rowell, UK, 1989.

'Joy Bielby'

This is an excellent lax, self-branching cultivar giving a good show in hanging baskets and hanging containers, inheriting its characteristics from its parents, 'Swingtime' and 'Blush o' Dawn'. The double flowers are medium to large with a white-streaked red tube, white sepals blushed with pink, tipped green and a white corolla flushed rose. The foliage is mid-green. Half hardy; Zones 9–10. Bielby, UK, 1982.

'Janice Ann'

'Kathy Louise'

This US cultivar is excellent in hanging containers. It has quite vigorous trailing growth with dark green glossy leaves. It is not especially self-branching and therefore needs plenty of early pinching. The flowers are large doubles with a longish carmine-red tube, carmine sepals with green tips and a soft rose corolla. It is quite heat-tolerant. Half hardy; Zones 9–10. Antonelli, USA, 1963.

'Katy Elizabeth Ann'

This beautiful cultivar, a sister seedling to 'Lillian Annetts', is excellent in hanging baskets and hanging pots. The flowers are small doubles of near perfect form with a white tube, light rose sepals and a white corolla blushed with pink and rose shading. The growth is lax and self-branching with mid-green foliage. Like 'Lillian Annetts', it grows easily to make a nice, slightly weeping standard. Half hardy; Zones 9–10. Clark, UK, 1992.

'Kegworth Carnival'

This has the growth habit of a lax bush and is therefore ideal for hanging baskets and containers, or to grow as a pot plant with cane supports. The flowers are medium-sized doubles with a white tube,

'Kit Oxtoby'

long white sepals that are quite thin and a Tyrian-purple corolla changing to rose-purple as it ages. It has medium-sized mid-green foliage and is very floriferous. Half hardy; Zones 9–10. Smith, UK, 1990.

'Kit Oxtoby'

This has a good trailing habit, with medium to large double flowers. The tube is neyron-rose, as are the rather broad, horizontal

sepals, while the rose-coloured corolla has darker edges to the petals. It is a vigorous grower with medium-sized mid-green foliage, and is quite floriferous given the size of the flowers. Half hardy; Zones 9–10. Beilby and Oxtoby, UK, 1990.

'Kiwi'

This is a US cultivar with lax growth and an abundance of large double flowers. Each flower has a long greenish-white tube, white sepals with green tips and a rose-coloured corolla with pale pink splashes on the petals. The medium-sized mid-green serrated leaves provide a good foil for the flower colours and it is an excellent cultivar to use in mixed baskets. Half hardy; Zones 9–10. Tiret, USA, 1966.

'Kon Tiki'

This floriferous cultivar has rather wiry growth with small to medium dark green leaves and makes a nice hanging pot, but is also amenable to growing in baskets and containers. The medium double flowers have a white tube, white sepals flushed pink and a violet corolla with pink patches at the base of the petals. It is not the easiest cultivar to find, but is well worth the search. Half hardy; Zones 9–10. Tiret, USA, 1965.

'Kegworth Carnival'

'Kon Tiki'

'La Campanella'

This free-flowering cultivar is very versatile, with wiry trailing self-branching growth with small mid-green leaves. It is best to pinch it well early on. It is good in hanging baskets, hanging pots and containers, and will also make an attractive small standard. The flowers are small to medium semi-doubles, with a white tube, white sepals flushed pink and an imperial purple corolla that matures to magenta. It has been widely used for hybridization, especially in the Netherlands. Half hardy; Zones 9–10. Blackwell, UK, 1968.

'Lady in Grey'

This makes a lax, bushy shape with mid-green serrated leaves, and you can use it in hanging baskets or containers. It is tricky to grow, needs a cool area and is quite late to flower, but the unusual colour combination is well worth the effort. The flowers are large doubles with a greenish-white tube, white sepals flushed pink with green tips and a grey-blue to mauve corolla, maturing to lavender, with pink veins and splashes on the petals. Half hardy; Zones 9–10. Lockerbie, Australia, 1988.

'Lady Kathleen Spence'

This is a very pretty cultivar with wiry lax growth, making it easy to grow in hanging containers, and it is also useful

'Lady Kathleen Spence'

for weeping standards or trained shapes. The flowers are medium-sized singles with a white tube blushed with pale pink, long thin sepals that are rose-white on top and darker underneath, and a pale lavender corolla fading to light lilac. It is very free-flowering with medium-sized mid-green foliage. Half hardy; Zones 9–10. Ryle, UK, 1974.

'Land van Beveren'

This vigorous sun-loving trailing cultivar does well in all sorts of hanging containers, and grows extremely well in a half basket.

An easy plant for the beginner to grow, it is very floriferous and has medium single flowers with a long waxy white tube, waxy white sepals and a dark carmine corolla. The foliage is medium-sized and mid-green. It is vigorous enough to make a good half or full weeping standard. Half hardy; Zones 9–10. Saintenoy, Netherlands, 1988.

'Lovely Linda'

This cultivar has a lax self-branching habit. It is easy to grow and ideal for hanging pots and baskets. The flower is a medium-sized single with a waxy white tube and sepals and a rose pink corolla. The growth is vigorous and it is very free-flowering, the flowers standing out nicely on the mid-green foliage. Half hardy; Zones 9–10. Allsop, UK, 1998.

'Mancunian'

This is an excellent cultivar to use in hanging baskets, especially mixed baskets, because of its good trailing habit, strong vigorous growth and attractive light to mid-green foliage. The flowers are medium to large doubles with a white tube striped with red, white recurving sepals and a full white corolla with red veins and a red blush at the base of the petals. The large, white pointed buds add to the beauty of this plant. Half hardy; Zones 9–10. Goulding, UK, 1985.

'Land van Beveren'

'Mancunian'

'Marinka'

'Marinka'

This fuchsia, hybridized more than 100 years ago, is still a popular cultivar grown the world over. It was first thought to have originated in France in 1902, but now it seems it came from Germany some years earlier. It does not have many faults, but the main one is the tendency for the leaves to mark and turn red with sudden changes in temperature, for instance when moving it out of the greenhouse. The flowers are single, almost a self-red with a red tube, red sepals initially cupping the corolla and eventually held just below the horizontal, and a dull red corolla. The pretty flowers and buds look superb held in the mid-green foliage and the growth is naturally trailing, easily making an excellent hanging basket. This one is also worth growing as a weeping half standard. Half hardy; Zones 9–10. Stika, Germany, 1890.

'Mood Indigo'

This is an unusual cultivar, strong-growing and extremely floriferous, and is suitable for hanging baskets or containers. The medium-sized double flower has a light yellowish-green tube with red blush, yellowish-green recurving sepals, red at the base, and a deep mauve corolla with an indigo tinge, pink at the petal base and splashed with red. The foliage is mid-green on top, yellowish-green underneath, and it has a lax but rather untidy growth habit. Half hardy; Zones 9–10. de Graaff, Netherlands, 1987.

'Mother's Day'

This Australian cultivar is a natural trailer, and has large, freely produced double flowers with a green tube striped white, white sepals with yellowish-green tips and a full corolla of frilled petals opening creamy-white and maturing to white. The foliage is dark green on the upper surface and lighter green underneath. It makes an excellent basket plant and is a good choice if you want a very large white double to grow in mixed containers with darker fuchsias. Half hardy; Zone 10. Richardson, Australia, 1988.

'Mood Indigo'

'Multa'

This cultivar is a small-flowered single with a red tube, red sepals and a mauve-purple corolla. It is very easy to grow, and definitely a good one for a beginner to try, with lax growth and medium-sized mid- to dark green foliage. It is very free-flowering over a long period. As well as being an excellent half basket plant covered with flowers, it also makes a good standard with a lax habit, and is effective in mixed planting in any kind of container. Half hardy; Zones 9–10. van Suchtelen, Netherlands, 1968.

'Normandy Bell'

This trailing cultivar makes a lax bush with rather long, light green leaves with serrated edges. The flowers are medium-sized singles with a short pale pink tube with darker stripes, long, broad, pinkish-white sepals tipped green and a light blue bell-shaped corolla with pink veining. It prefers some shade to full sun. Half hardy; Zones 9–10. Martin, USA, 1961.

'Novella'

This pretty fuchsia has medium-sized semi-double flowers with a long flesh-pink tube, long rosy-pink sepals and a salmon-orange corolla. The growth is rather lax, with medium-sized, mid-green serrated foliage. It grows very well in hanging baskets, hanging pots and containers, and makes an attractive weeping standard. Half hardy; Zone 10. Tiret, USA, 1967.

'Novella'

'Orange Drops'

'Orange King'

'Orange Drops'
This cultivar has one of the best orange colours and is suitable for basket or weeping standard training. It has the growth habit of a lax bush, with serrated mid-green leaves that can grow very large if overfed early in the season. The flowers are medium-sized singles with a long, light orange tube, light orange sepals and a dark orange corolla, which is slightly iridescent. The flowers tend to display and hang together in clusters. Half hardy; Zones 9–10. Martin, USA, 1963.

'Orange King'
One a group of orange-flowered cultivars, this makes an excellent fuchsia for hanging baskets because of its trailing habit. It has medium to large double flowers with a white tube blushed pale pink, pale pink arching sepals and a very full corolla that opens orange, maturing to smoky salmon-pink with orange splashes. The serrated foliage is mid-green, and the contrasting flower colour makes it quite striking. Half hardy; Zones 9–10. Wright, UK, 1975.

'Ovation'
This fuchsia is beautiful for hanging baskets and larger hanging pots. The medium-sized double flowers have a long ivory tube with faint pink stripes, broad horizontal ivory sepals with a pink flush

and a full deep red corolla. The trailing growth has quite large mid-green leaves and it is reasonably free-flowering. Half hardy; Zones 9–10. Stubbs, USA, 1981.

'Panique'
This relatively new introduction is quite small-growing, but has a tremendous quantity of small single flowers. The tube is pink, the sepals are orchid-pink and the corolla is a deeper pink. The foliage is also

small to medium in size and mid-green in colour. With its compact growth, this plant is excellent for a smaller hanging basket or for use in mixed containers. Half hardy; Zones 9–10. de Graaff, Netherlands, 2000.

'Patricia Ann'
This is a vigorous trailer, ideal for hanging baskets. It tolerates heat if shaded, and has rather large mid-green leaves. The large double flowers have a long neyron-rose tube with pink stripes, long white sepals with a pale pink stripe above and darker pink beneath and a full neyron-rose corolla, with a paler colour at the base of the petals, which are veined dark pink. Half hardy; Zones 9–10. Clements, UK, 1982.

'Pink Galore'
This is one of the best pinks in the group of trailing cultivars. The flowers are medium-sized doubles with a medium-length pale pink tube, long pale pink sepals tipped green swept upwards and a pale candy-pink corolla. The abundant flowers stand out well against the rather glossy, ovate, dark green leaves. It is not the most vigorous of cultivars, so use one or two extra plants when planting a hanging basket. Half hardy; Zones 9–10. Fuchsia-La, USA, 1951.

'Pink Galore'

'Pink Marshmallow'

'Postiljon'

'Pink Marshmallow'

This strong-growing trailing cultivar has very large double flowers with a long pale pink tube, broad pale pink reflexing sepals and a full white corolla with loose, pink-veined petals with some pink blushing, depending on the amount of sun. The medium to large foliage is light green. It makes a very impressive hanging basket or can be used in mixed containers for its stunning flowers. In common with many double whites, it is prone to botrytis, so water carefully early in the season. Half hardy; Zones 9–10. Stubbs, USA, 1977.

'Postiljon'

This vigorous self-branching and trailing cultivar is well worth growing, an easy choice for the beginner. It is early-flowering and makes a good basket quickly. Its small single flowers have a short white tube flushed pink, and broad cream-white sepals flushed rose, held out over the rosy-purple corolla. The flowers contrast well with the small mid-green foliage as it hangs down from containers. It is also good for hanging pots, mixed containers and small weeping standards. Half hardy; Zones 9–10. van der Post, Netherlands, 1975.

'President Margaret Slater'

A seedling from 'Cascade', this has a similar growth habit and is named after a former president of the British Fuchsia Society. The true cascading growth habit and medium-sized dark green serrated foliage make it ideal for hanging containers, especially the mixed ones. The flowers are medium-sized singles with a white tube, white sepals flushed with pink and tipped green and a mauve corolla with a salmon-pink blush. It is very floriferous, tolerates heat and develops the best flower colours in the sun. Half hardy; Zones 9–10. Taylor, UK, 1972.

'Princessita'

This older variety of fuchsia is still widely grown because it is very free-flowering over a long period. It has strong trailing growth with medium-sized mid- to dark green foliage and medium-sized single flowers with a white tube, long, narrow white upturned sepals flushed pink underneath, and a deep rose-pink corolla. It makes excellent full or half baskets, and is also a good cultivar for filling containers. Half hardy; Zones 9–10. Niederholzer, USA, 1940.

'Quasar'

This is a large-growing, spreading lax double, trailing owing to the size and weight of the flowers. The medium to large double flowers have a white tube, white sepals and a compact dauphin-violet corolla with white patches at the base of the petals. The medium to large foliage is light green and contrasts well with the unusual flower colours. This plant is very good for growing in mixed containers. Half hardy; Zones 9–10. Walker, USA, 1974.

'Queen of Hearts'

This cultivar is good in hanging baskets because of the large double flowers with a short carmine tube, flaring broad carmine sepals and a full corolla with violet-purple centre petals and carmine pink outer petals. Note that there is an upright bushy single cultivar with the same name raised by Tabraham in 1974 , so check which one it is before buying. Half hardy; Zones 9–10. Kennett, USA, 1961.

'Quasar'

'Red Shadows'

'Red Shadows'

This is a lax cultivar from the US Waltz stable, with rather unusual flowers in a very nice colour combination. The large double flowers have a crimson tube and crimson sepals, which cup the dark burgundy-purple corolla, with crimson at the base of the petals. The flowers change colour as they mature, finally becoming a ruby-red. The foliage is mid-green with red veins. The growth is best classed as a lax bush, so it can be used in a hanging basket or as a pot plant with support. Half hardy; Zones 9–10. Waltz, USA, 1962.

'Red Spider'

This superbly floriferous fuchsia is very vigorous and makes quite long, stiff trailing growth with mid-green foliage, but it does not self-branch and needs a lot of pinching out early on. The medium-sized single flowers have a long crimson tube and sepals, and a rose corolla. It is an excellent cultivar, good for mixed baskets and containers. Note that it has nothing in common with, nor any special predilection towards the pest of the same name. Half hardy; Zones 9–10. Reiter, USA, 1946.

'Roesse Blacky'

'Roesse Blacky' ('Blacky')

This relatively new introduction from the Roesse stable, commonly marketed with the name 'Blacky', has a quite startling colour. The medium semi-double flowers have a red tube and sepals and a deep purple corolla that is almost black when it first opens. The foliage is small to medium in size and mid-green in colour, and the growth is lax and arching. It is very good for use in containers and baskets, particularly when viewing the flowers at eye level. You could also try growing this fuchsia as a weeping standard, as its manner of growth is quite suitable for this shape. Half hardy; Zones 9–10. Roes, Netherlands, 2002.

'Ronald L. Lockerbie'

When first introduced, this was promoted as the first yellow fuchsia, although it is actually more of a creamy white. It had the honour of being named after Ronald Lockerbie, a prolific Australian hybridizer of fuchsias. The flower is a medium-sized double with a cream tube flushed carmine, white sepals and a cream to pale yellow corolla, fading to white. The foliage is medium-sized and light green, with quite long joints between the leaf nodes. This plant grows well in baskets and containers. Half hardy; Zones 9–10. Richardson, Australia, 1986.

'Ruby Wedding'

This is a good choice if you want large double flowers with an unusual colour for a hanging basket. The medium-length tube is ruby, the ruby sepals are quite broad and semi-reflexed, and the full corolla is red with overtones of orange and mauve. It is quite floriferous for the size of the flowers and grows strongly with arching stems and large mid-green foliage. It is an ideal gift for those couples reaching that landmark. Half hardy; Zones 9–10. Forward, UK, 1990.

'Ruth King'

This is a stiff trailing fuchsia with medium-sized mid-green foliage. The medium to large double flowers have a pink tube and sepals and a lilac and white compact corolla. This cultivar is very suitable for growing in the centre of mixed baskets and containers and is well worth trying as a weeping standard. Half hardy; Zones 9–10. Tiret, USA, 1967.

'Ruby Wedding'

'Seventh Heaven'

'Southgate'

'Seventh Heaven'

This naturally trailing cultivar has medium to large double flowers, a white tube with green streaks, white sepals shading to pink and a full orange-red corolla. It is an eye-catching and very floriferous fuchsia, with mid-green foliage and arching growth. It makes a nice basket on its own, but is also excellent in mixed hanging containers. The flowers are at their best when viewed from eye level or slightly below, and for this reason it is another fuchsia that looks superb grown as a weeping standard. It should be in everyone's collection. Half hardy; Zones 9–10. Stubbs, USA, 1981.

'Sophisticated Lady'

The trailing growth habit of this fuchsia makes it very suitable for hanging baskets. The medium to large double flowers have a short pale pink tube, long and quite broad pale pink sepals, and a short, full white corolla. The small to medium-sized serrated foliage is mid-green with red veining. Half hardy; Zones 9–10. Martin, USA, 1964.

'Southgate'

This grows in the manner of a lax bush with mid-green foliage, and is ideal for hanging baskets or as a pot plant with supports. The striking flowers are medium-sized doubles with a pink tube, pink sepals that are paler above and darker underneath, and a powder-pink fluffy corolla with pink veining on the petals. Because of its slightly stiff habit of growth it can be trained in various ways, for example as a standard or even a fan. Half hardy; Zones 9–10. Walker and Jones, USA, 1951.

'Susan Green'

This is a very pretty trailing cultivar with strong, self-branching growth and medium-sized mid-green foliage. The flowers are medium-sized singles with a pale pink tube, pale pink sepals with green tips and a coral-pink corolla. It can be grown as an excellent hanging pot plant or in a hanging basket, and is equally at home in a hanging container with mixed plants. It also makes a superb weeping half standard. Half hardy; Zones 9–10. Caunt, UK, 1981.

'Swingtime'

This superb fuchsia is grown by many gardeners and has been consistently popular for many years. It is a classic basket fuchsia against which many other trailing cultivars are judged. The flowers are double and medium to large with a red tube, red sepals and a very full, fluffy white corolla with red veining on the petals. The foliage is on the small side, mid- to dark green with red veining, and the growth is vigorous, wiry and trailing. It does very well in any type of basket or container, and can also be grown as an excellent weeping full or half standard. Half hardy; Zones 9–10. Tiret, USA, 1950.

'Sylvia Barker'

This fuchsia has rather small flowers but they are numerous, with a long waxy white tube, waxy white sepals with green tips and a smoky-red corolla. The colours are quite distinctive and stand out well against the dark green leaves. It makes an arching, lax trailing plant that is excellent when grown in a half basket or hanging pot. This cultivar also grows very well in mixed containers and makes a superb weeping standard. Half hardy; Zones 9–10. Barker, UK, 1973.

'Susan Green'

'Taffeta Bow'

Excellent for hanging baskets, this cultivar has distinctive medium to large double flowers with a short pink tube, long carmine-rose sepals and a purple-violet corolla with serrated petal edges and pink splashes. As the fuchsias mature, the petals develop an unusual curved shape, which is what gives it its name. It has good vigorous growth with dark green foliage and an abundance of flowers. Half hardy; Zones 9–10. Stubbs, USA, 1974.

'Tom West'

This very old and adaptable cultivar has a number of different uses, including hanging baskets and pots. The flowers are small to medium-sized singles with a carmine tube and sepals, and a purple corolla. It has very attractive variegated foliage with patches of green, cream and cerise, becoming redder in the sun. The growth is rather wiry and spreading but it grows well in a basket, particularly a half basket, and is also good when trained as a standard or used in summer bedding schemes. Frost hardy; Zones 7–8. Meillez, France, 1853.

'Tom West'

'Trailing Queen'

This old German cultivar has vigorous, long trailing growth and is very floriferous, though it can suffer from premature flower drop when conditions are too hot and dry. The flowers are medium-sized singles with a thin red tube and red sepals, and the corolla opens a red-violet and matures to a dull red. The unusual foliage is bronze-green with red veining in the leaves, and the buds add to the attraction, changing colour as they grow. Half hardy; Zones 9–10. Kohene, Germany, 1896.

'Trudi Davro'

This is a relatively new trailing fuchsia, a good addition to the range of whites. The flowers are a medium double with a pale pink tube and sepals and a full white corolla that stands out within the small to medium-sized bright green foliage. The pink colouring of the flower becomes more intense when grown in the sun. It makes a superb hanging pot, but is also well worth using in baskets or other hanging containers mixed with fuchsias of other colours. Half hardy; Zones 9–10. Raiser unknown, UK, introduction date unknown.

'Veenlust'

'University of Liverpool'

'University of Liverpool'

This newer cultivar is excellent for hanging baskets with its vigorous lax growth, and it flowers well over a long period. The flowers are medium-sized singles with a white tube and sepals, and a red bell-shaped corolla, with up to three flowers growing from each leaf axil. The foliage is mid- to dark green, contrasting well with the flowers. It is well worth trying as a weeping standard. Half hardy; Zones 9–10. Clark, UK, 1998.

'Veenlust'

This lax cultivar is a good choice for hanging pots, hanging baskets and mixed containers. The medium to large double flowers have a medium-length white tube, white sepals with green tips and a full bright red corolla, some of the petals with pink splashes. The inner petals can sometimes grow in a lower ring, giving a very deep corolla with structural similarities to 'Two Tiers'. The foliage is mid-green and the growth vigorous and lax, though not very self-branching. Half hardy; Zones 9–10. Jansink, Netherlands, 1994.

'Walsingham'

This is a stunningly beautiful cultivar with pastel flowers and rather bright green foliage. It has the habit of a lax bush with semi-trailing growth, and it is very effective in all types of raised containers, especially half baskets and hanging pots. The flowers are medium-sized semi-doubles with a pale pink tube and sepals, and a pale lavender-lilac corolla. Some catalogues list it as a double but it is really a semi-double with some double flowers. Take care not to overwater, because it can be prone to botrytis early in the season. Half hardy; Zones 9–10. Clithero, UK, 1979.

'Wave of Life'

This is an old cultivar, probably grown more for its foliage than its flowers. It has small to medium-sized single flowers with a scarlet tube and sepals, and a magenta-purple corolla. It bears splendid greenish-yellow and gold leaves, while the growth is lax but not especially vigorous. Probably best used in hanging pots or mixed containers for its leaf colour. Half hardy; Zones 9–10. Henderson, UK, 1896.

'Wendy's Beauty'

This beautiful trailing cultivar has large double flowers with a white tube and long white sepals flushed with rose, and an unusually coloured violet to pale purple full

'Wilson's Pearls'

corolla. The flowers are produced very freely for such a large double and the lax growth has dark yellowish-green leaves, among which the flowers stand out well. Half hardy; Zones 9–10. Garrett, USA, 1989.

'Wilson's Pearls'

This is a floriferous trailing cultivar with pale to mid-green foliage, ideal in hanging baskets or pots and all kinds of raised containers. The flowers are medium-sized singles with a medium length red tube,

red sepals that curl back and twist, and a white corolla veined red. The petals often become blushed pink when grown in the sun. This one is easy to grow and is widely available. Half hardy; Zones 9–10. Wilson, UK, 1967.

'Windhapper'

This is a fine cascading Dutch cultivar, excellent for hanging baskets and elevated containers with its large, bright mid-green leaves with a distinctive red central vein. It has large single flowers with a short greenish-white tube, long white sepals with a pink blush and green tips, and a violet corolla with lighter colour at the petal base. The best flower colours develop in areas with more shade. Half hardy; Zones 9–10. Moerman, Netherlands, 1991.

'Zulu King'

This is a cultivar for those looking for a very dark coloured fuchsia to grow in a basket or hanging pot. The medium-sized single flowers have a deep carmine tube and sepals, and a dark black-purple corolla that holds its dark colour well through to maturity. It has good trailing growth and rather dark green foliage. Grow it where the flowers are easy to see. Half hardy; Zones 9–10. de Graaff, Netherlands, 1990.

'Wendy's Beauty'

'Zulu King'

Triphylla fuchsias

These hybrids all need winter protection in temperate areas. They need minimum temperatures of 10°C (50°F) to grow on in green leaf through the winter and 5°C (41°F) to overwinter in a dormant state. Cooler than this, the spring growth is delayed a few weeks.

'Adinda'

This fairly new cultivar is a slightly smaller variety than many older Triphylla hybrids, with beautiful small single flowers growing in terminal clusters, the flowers being a salmon-pink self. The foliage is an attractive shade of sage green, with upright growth. It makes an excellent pot plant and a great summer bedder. Tender; Zone 11. Dijkstra, Netherlands, 1995.

'Andenken an Heinrich Henkel' ('Heinrich Henkel')

This is a beautiful lax Triphylla, with medium rose-crimson flowers growing in terminal clusters. The flowers make a beautiful contrast to the large dark green foliage, and it tolerates full sun quite happily. It grows well as a lax pot plant, but be careful not to overwater it. Try it in a hanging basket or as a lax standard. Tender; Zone 11. Berger, Germany, 1896.

'Billy Green'

This popular cultivar is a Triphylla type rather than a true Triphylla, which means the flowers grow from the leaf axils rather than in terminal racemes. The flower is a Triphylla shape, albeit a little fatter. The flower is a salmon-pink self colour and the growth vigorous and upright, with lovely olive-sage-green foliage. It makes an excellent specimen plant in a single season of growth. This is one for a patio because it happily stands full sun. Try using it as a summer bedder as well. Frost tender; Zones 10–11. Raiser unknown, UK, 1962.

'Bornemann's Beste'

This strong-growing fuchsia is a Triphylla type suitable for use as a pot or bedding plant. The flowers are medium-sized orange-red singles with long tubes, growing mainly in terminal clusters. Current opinion states that this fuchsia is the same as the one named 'Georg Bornemann' in Germany. Tender; Zone 11. Bonstedt, Germany, 1904.

'Chantry Park'

Unlike most Triphyllas, this cultivar has short-jointed, bushy and slightly lax growth with medium mid- to olive green foliage. It is still truly terminal-flowering, with medium-sized flowers in terminal clusters. The flowers have a scarlet tube

'Billy Green'

and sepals and a bright scarlet corolla, the sepals and corolla being a little larger in proportion to the tube than the average Triphylla. It grows very well in a hanging pot or basket, and is very suitable for a wall pot. Tender; Zone 11. Stannard, UK, 1991.

'Coralle' ('Koralle')

This cultivar resulted from the work of the German hybridizer Carl Bonstedt, and is also known by the alternative German spelling 'Koralle'. It is a strong, upright grower with medium-sized flowers produced in terminal clusters. The flowers are orange-red self-coloured, with large, deep sage green, velvety foliage. Tender; Zones 10–11. Bonstedt, Germany, 1905.

'Adinda'

'Coralle'

'Edwin Goulding'

This is an upright and bushy fuchsia with medium-sized Triphylla flowers in terminal clusters, with a darkish red tube and sepals, and a brighter red corolla. It has medium to dark green foliage that contrasts well with the flower colour. Tender; Zone 11. Stannard, UK, 1992.

'Elfriede Ott'

This fuchsia is rather unusual because of its stiff, spreading upright growth that will make a tall plant. The distinctive flowers, which grow in terminal clusters, have a slightly bent salmon-pink tube and sepals, and a darker salmon-pink corolla. The four curled and folded petals give the appearance of a semi-double and the stamens almost hide in the flowers. The medium-sized dark green foliage is a perfect foil to the salmon-pink flowers. This fuchsia resulted from a hybridization cross between 'Coralle' and *F. splendens*. Frost tender; Zone 11. Nutzinger, Austria, 1976.

'Firecracker'

This Triphylla is a truly variegated sport from 'Thalia', which is now widely grown. It flowers in terminal clusters, as does 'Thalia', and the medium flowers are orange-scarlet self-coloured, but it has beautiful leaves with a startling olive green and cream variegation with traces of red. Use it in pots or as a summer bedder, but be aware that it needs growing on the dry side or you will lose it to botrytis. This cultivar is subject to breeder's rights protection. Tender; Zone 11. Fuchsiavale, UK, 1987.

'Fred Swales'

The stiff and lax growth habit of this fuchsia looks very effective in hanging baskets and containers. The flowers are borne in terminal clusters and have a reddish-orange tube and sepals with a corolla that opens orange with a purple edge to the petals that matures to orange. The foliage is mid-green above and lighter underneath, with red veining and stems, while the mature branches are brown. Tender; Zones 10–11. Bielby and Oxtoby, UK, 1988.

'Elfriede Ott'

'Gartenmeister Bonstedt'

This is one of Carl Bonstedt's superb Triphylla cultivars. The flowers appear in terminal clusters, being orange-red with a long tube. They are very similar to 'Thalia' but have a more pronounced bulge in the tube. The strong, upright bushy growth has a covering of bronze-green foliage. Heat and sun are not a problem, and this Triphylla makes an excellent summer bedding and specimen pot plant. In a greenhouse, it will continue flowering well into the winter. Frost tender; Zones 10–11. Bonstedt, Germany, 1905.

'Insulinde'

This is a newer Triphylla hybrid, with strong, upright growth and startling dark green shiny foliage. The medium-sized flowers are borne in terminal clusters, with a tomato-red tube, sepals that are tomato-red on the topside and vermilion-pink on the underside, and a tomato-red corolla. It is a strong growing plant, naturally quite self-branching, and the colour combination makes it a welcome addition to the range. It makes a very nice pot plant and grows well as a summer bedder. Frost tender; Zone 11. de Graaff, Netherlands, 1991.

'Gartenmeister Bonstedt'

'Insulinde'

'Jackqueline'

'Orient Express'

'Jackqueline'

This Triphylla cultivar has terminal clusters of medium flowers with a scarlet tube and sepals, and an orange corolla. It has good upright growth with dark green velvety leaves, and is happy in full sun. Use it as a pot plant or a striking specimen plant. Tender; Zone 11. Oxtoby, UK, 1987.

'Mantilla'

This fuchsia is a very interesting Triphylla type, excellent when used in hanging baskets and pots. It has strong, vigorous and pendant growth with lovely dark green

'Mantilla'

foliage. The flowers are borne in terminal clusters and have long rich carmine tubes, short light carmine sepals and a vermilion corolla. The corolla is unusually large and well exposed beneath the sepals. It grows best in a well-lit, warm position and makes an excellent half basket. Tender; Zone 11. Reiter, USA, 1948.

'Mary'

This is another of Carl Bonstedt's raisings, and arguably one of the best Triphyllas in cultivation. It bears its medium-sized vivid crimson self-coloured flowers in terminal clusters. The tube is distinctly slimmer at the top and widens close to the flower. The growth is upright, self-branching and slightly lax, with large velvety leaves that are a beautiful shade of sage green. It is quite happy in full sun and makes an excellent specimen plant. It will also make a nice, slightly lax quarter or half standard, though great care is needed when growing the stem, because of the terminal-flowering habit. If it starts to flower while you are growing the stem, it will not grow any higher. Frost tender; Zone 11. Bonstedt, Germany, 1897.

'Obergartner Koch'

This is a strong upright cultivar with large, red-veined olive-green leaves, suitable as a pot plant or for summer bedding. The

flowers are borne in terminal clusters with a long bright orange tube, which is very thin at the top, with a pronounced bulge before the sepals. The sepals and corolla are also bright orange. Tender; Zone 11. Sauer, Germany, 1912.

'Orient Express'

This has strong upright growth and needs hard pinching in the early stages to make a well-shaped plant. It has quite unusually coloured flowers, borne in terminal clusters, with a long pink tube striped with darker pink, red-tipped pale pink-white sepals and a rose-pink corolla. It has large mid-green leaves which, when combined with the flowers and buds, makes it an interesting addition to the range of Triphyllas. Frost tender; Zone 11. Goulding, UK, 1985.

'Our Ted'

The first-ever white-flowered Triphylla cultivar, this was named after Ted Stiff, a great fuchsia personality in the east of England. The growth is upright, with terminal clusters of medium white self-coloured flowers, though the corolla petals can have a touch of pink. The foliage is dark green and quite glossy. This cultivar is one for the experienced gardener because it is not easy to grow. Tender; Zone 11. Goulding, UK, 1987.

'Roos Breytenbach'

This is a strong-growing, slightly lax upright with terminal clusters of long scarlet flowers. The sepals are long for a Triphylla, and the corolla rather different with the petals pleated together to form an unusual shape. The foliage is mid- to dark green and slightly more of an ovate shape than other Triphylla hybrids. This cultivar is excellent in hanging baskets and containers. Tender; Zone 11. Stannard, UK, 1993.

'Sparky'

This new Triphylla cultivar is unusual in that the small flowers are thrown outwards and upwards in terminal clusters. The tube and sepals are dark blood-red, as is the corolla. It has upright growth and is short-jointed and very bushy, with small to medium (for a Triphylla) dark green leaves. It grows well as a pot plant and makes a good quarter standard. It does well growing in a conservatory. Tender; Zone 11. Webb, UK, 1994.

'Stella Ann'

This is a vigorous upright and self-branching cultivar that is extremely floriferous, with dark olive green leaves with purple ribs and veins. The flowers, held in huge terminal clusters, have a thick poppy-red tube, poppy-red sepals with green tips and an Indian orange corolla.

'Sparky'

This is an excellent choice for growing as a smaller specimen pot plant or in a summer bedding scheme. Tender; Zone 11. Dunnet, UK, 1974.

'Thalia'

This is probably the best-known Triphylla hybrid. It has strong upright growth with medium-sized, orange-scarlet self-coloured flowers borne in terminal clusters. The dark olive-green foliage shows the flowers off very well. Often used in public bedding schemes, where it makes a good show, it can also form an excellent specimen

plant and a good quarter or half standard. Once it starts flowering it does not stop until you have to cut it back in autumn. Frost tender; Zones 10–11. Bonstedt, Germany, 1905.

'Traudchen Bonstedt'

This beautiful Triphylla is one that should be more widely grown. It has single flowers in terminal clusters with a long, light salmon-pink tube and short sepals of the same colour. The corolla is light orange with white anthers and a pale salmon pistil that almost hides in the flower. The light sage-green leaves have a velvety texture with a reddish tint underneath. To ensure the plant's survival over winter, it should be kept in green leaf rather than allowed to go dormant. Tender; Zone 11. Bonstedt, Germany, 1905.

'Whiteknights Cheeky'

This smaller Triphylla is very suitable for pots, with its small flowers held horizontally in terminal clusters. The flowers are a single main colour, described as either Tyrian-purple or red-aubergine. The colour varies depending on the conditions in which the plant is grown, and is best when grown in full sun. The attractive foliage is small and dark green with a velvety texture. The plant originated from an interspecies cross between *F. triphylla* and *F. procumbens*. Frost tender; Zone 11. Wright, UK, 1980.

'Thalia'

'Whiteknights Cheeky'

Fuchsias in pots

Excellent plants for growing in pots, fuchsias can be used for brightening up dark corners around the garden, for displays or for exhibition. Free-flowering varieties, which possess an upright and self-branching habit of growth, are the best types to use.

'Abigail Reine'
The first part of the name of this cultivar is variously spelt as 'Abigale', 'Abigayle', 'Abigayles' and 'Abbigayle' in different catalogues. It is the best variegated sport from 'Rose Fantasia', with mid-green leaves with bright yellow variegation. The flower is identical to that of 'Rose Fantasia', a medium-sized single, upward-facing with a deep pink tube and sepals, and a pale pink corolla with a hint of mauve. It makes an attractive pot plant, but you should keep it in as much light as possible to enhance the foliage colours. Half hardy; Zones 9–10. Hunton, UK, 1998.

'Alaska'
This is a good upright that grows with strong stems and striking, large white double flowers with a white tube, white sepals tipped green and a very full, fluffy

'Abigail Reine'

'Alberttina'

white corolla. The foliage is dark green, and when in full flower there is some arching of the stems caused by the weight of the flowers. It is well worth growing as a half or full standard, and ideal for placing in dull corners where the white flowers stand out. It is an excellent addition to any collection. Half hardy; Zones 9–10. Schnabel, USA, 1963.

'Alberttina' ('Albertina')
This strong-growing, self-branching plant will form a good bush or shrub with minimal shaping. The small to medium-sized single flowers have a white tube flushed rose, rose-flushed white reflexed sepals and a flared lavender-rose corolla. There is medium-sized mid- to dark green foliage. This fuchsia is free-flowering and makes a good pot plant or smaller standard. Try using it for summer bedding as well. Half hardy; Zones 9–10. Netjes, Netherlands, 1988.

'Atlantic Star'
The upright, self-branching, short-jointed growth of this fuchsia creates an excellent compact pot plant. The flowers are medium-sized singles with a cream-striped pink tube, white sepals blushed pink and a bell-shaped white corolla with faint pink veins. The medium-sized

mid-green leaves have a serrated edge and red stems, providing a perfect foil for the flowers. The plant is also excellent grown as a quarter standard. Half hardy; Zones 9–10. Redfern, UK, 1986.

'Bealings'
This is a good choice for growing as a medium-sized pot plant or small standard. The flowers are small to medium-sized doubles with a white tube and sepals, and the corolla is very full and dark violet, fading with age. The upright, short-jointed self-branching growth carries small mid-green leaves and plenty of flowers for a double cultivar. Half hardy; Zones 9–10. Goulding, UK, 1983.

'Ben Jammin'
This is a very pretty cultivar with compact, short-jointed growth, excellent when grown as a smaller pot plant or small standard. The distinctive, small to medium-sized single flowers have a pale pink tube, pink-flushed aubergine sepals, and a dark aubergine corolla that caused a stir when first released. The foliage is small to medium in size and mid- to dark green in colour. Many nurseries list this cultivar as hardy in their catalogues, but this has not been proven by any definitive trials. Half hardy; Zones 9–10. Carless, UK, 1998.

'Ben Jammin'

'Border Raider'

'Caspar Hauser'

'Border Raider'

This fuchsia has made a big impression in the exhibition world since its introduction. The prolific flowers are small to medium-sized semi-erect singles with a deep rose tube and sepals, and a white corolla with slightly scalloped edges to the petals. The growth is naturally shrub-like, with small to medium-sized light green leaves. It makes a very nice quarter standard or pot plant. It does not overwinter well in a dormant state, and is better to keep in green leaf if possible. Half hardy; Zones 9–10. Gordon, UK, 2001.

'Brookwood Belle'

This strong, upright bushy cultivar is excellent for pot plants and is popular as an exhibition plant, having been in the top-ten list for some years. The flowers are medium-sized doubles with a deep cerise tube and sepals, and a pink-flushed white corolla veined red. The medium-sized foliage is bright mid-green. It is very floriferous and has a long period of flowering. Half hardy; Zones 9–10. Gilbert, UK, 1988.

'Cambridge Louie'

This cultivar should be in everyone's collection as it is a vigorous grower and will easily form a large pot plant covered in flowers. It is best to grow it in direct sun, as long as you can keep the roots cool;

the sun encourages it to produce harder wood that is not so likely to collapse under the weight of flowers. The medium single flowers have a pink-orange tube and sepals and a rosy-pink corolla, and they stand out well on the small, light green foliage. Half hardy; Zones 9–10. Napthen, UK, 1977.

'Caspar Hauser'

This cultivar is worth growing for its unusual flower colours. The growth is spreading, upright and self-branching, with light to mid-green foliage. It is a vigorous plant and quickly makes an

impressive shrub. The flowers are small to medium-sized doubles with a cardinal red tube and sepals, and a rather tight ruby-red corolla with lighter red patches at the base of the petals. Try it in baskets or containers as a centre plant as they will benefit from its lax but stiff upright growth. Half hardy; Zones 9–10. Springer, Germany, 1987.

'Cloverdale Pearl'

This fuchsia is very easy to grow as a pot plant, with its upright, self-branching growth and small mid- to dark green leaves. The flower is a medium-sized single with a white tube, pale pink sepals with green tips and a white corolla with red veining on the petals. You can grow this cultivar as a summer bedder or train it as a standard and various other shapes. Half hardy; Zones 9–10. Gadsby, UK, 1974.

'Cotton Candy'

This good strong upright-growing cultivar will make a nice shrub with medium-sized double flowers with a white tube, white sepals flushed pink and a fluffy pale pink corolla with cerise veins. The medium to large mid- to dark green leaves make a good foil for the flowers, which are freely produced for a double. It will make a large plant quite quickly, so it is also possible to grow it as a half standard. Half hardy; Zones 9–10. Tiret, USA, 1994.

'Cotton Candy'

'Delta's Sara'

'Doris Joan'

'Delta's KO'

This vigorous upright will quickly make a large bush or shrub. The flowers are large doubles with a cream-coloured tube, cream sepals flushed rosy-purple, much darker beneath, and a deep purple corolla. The combination of the medium-sized and mid- to dark green foliage with the flowers gives a striking overall effect. Half hardy; Zones 9–10. Vreeke and van't Westeinde, Netherlands, 1994.

'Delta's Sara'

This is a strong-growing, upright, floriferous Dutch cultivar with medium-sized semi-double flowers. They have a white tube and sepals, and a bluish-purple flared corolla with pink patches on the petals set against medium-sized mid-green leaves. It needs early pinching out to improve the bushiness, and easily makes a bush, medium-sized standard or bedding plant. Some nurseries claim it is hardy, but this has not been proven by any definitive trials. Half hardy; Zones 9–10. van't Westeinde, Netherlands, 2002.

'Doris Joan'

This is a strong-growing upright with mid- to dark green, slightly glossy leaves and rather unusual flowers. They are small

to medium-sized singles with a cream and carmine tube, cream and carmine reflexed sepals with green tips and a pale pink and lavender corolla with pronounced scalloped edges to the petals, giving the flower its distinctive shape. Half hardy; Zones 9–10. Sheppard, UK, 1997.

'Dulcie Elizabeth'

This is an excellent cultivar for growing in pots, with upright, bushy, self-branching growth and medium-sized mid-green foliage. The flowers are medium-sized doubles with a rose tube and sepals, and a full blue corolla with pink splashes, the outer petals being lighter than the inner ones. This variety tends to be a slightly late flowerer, but the attractive flowers are well worth the wait. Half hardy; Zones 9–10. Clyne and Aimes, UK, 1974.

'Eden Lady'

A sister seedling to 'Border Queen', this has similar growth, being upright, self-branching, bushy and short-jointed. It easily makes a superb bush or shrub. The flowers are medium-sized singles with a rose tube and sepals, and a hyacinth-blue corolla, and they stand out beautifully among the mid-green leaves. It is excellent as a half or quarter standard, and in summer bedding. Either 'Eden Lady' or 'Border Queen' should be in every beginner's collection. Half hardy; Zones 9–10. Ryle, UK, 1975.

'Eden Princess'

The medium to large single flowers of this fuchsia have a reddish-pink tube and sepals, and a mallow-purple corolla that contrasts beautifully with the golden foliage. New leaves at the growing tips have distinct red veining. The strong upright growth makes it ideal as a pot plant or standard. Half hardy; Zones 9–10. Mitcheson, UK, 1984.

'Eden Princess'

'Eleanor Leytham'

This cultivar has stiff upright and bushy growth with small glossy mid-green leaves. The profuse small semi-erect single flowers have a white flushed pink tube and sepals and a pink corolla with deeper coloured edges to the petals. This is an excellent plant for growing in smaller pot sizes or as smaller standards. Half hardy; Zones 9–10. Roe, UK, 1973.

'Estelle Marie'

This cultivar is one of the upward-flowering types. The flowers are small singles with a greenish-white tube, white sepals with green tips and a violet-blue corolla maturing to violet. It is extremely floriferous and has strong, stiff, short-jointed upright growth with light to mid-green foliage. Use it as a single specimen plant in an attractive pot or in mixed containers on the patio with other fuchsias or companion plants. It is also very effective when used as part of a summer bedding scheme, either individually or in blocks; the flowers look rather similar to little pansies, nodding in the breeze. Half hardy; Zones 9–10. Newton, UK, 1973.

'Finn'

This is a strong upright with a good bushy habit that responds well to pinching. The flowers are medium-sized singles with a longish ivory-white tube, ivory-white recurving sepals blushed pink and a long tubular corolla in an unusual shade of orange-red. The medium-sized, mid- to dark green foliage adds to the healthy look. This cultivar is excellent used as a pot plant, standard or summer bedder. Half hardy; Zones 9–10. Goulding, UK, 1988.

'Flying Cloud'

The large double flowers of this cultivar are very freely produced for their large size. Each flower has a white tube, white recurved sepals blushed rose underneath and a full white corolla that is pink at the base. The whole flower takes on a pinker tinge grown in full sun. 'Flying Cloud' makes a lax bush and may need some support when grown as a pot plant to help support the weight of the large blooms. It also makes a nice semi-weeping standard and can be used in containers. Half hardy; Zones 9–10. Reiter, USA, 1949.

'Forward Look'

This cultivar has upright and bushy growth with medium-sized mid-green foliage. The attractive medium-sized single flowers, held semi-erect, have a short china-rose tube, china-rose sepals tipped green and a wisteria-blue corolla fading to mauve. It is well suited to growing as a pot plant or medium-sized standard. Half hardy; Zones 9–10. Gadsby, UK, 1972.

'Flying Cloud'

'Frank Saunders'

This fuchsia has very pretty small single flowers with a white tube and sepals, and a small lilac-pink corolla. The flowers are semi-erect, tending to stand out from the foliage. The growth habit is upright, bushy and self-branching, with small dark green leaves. It forms a dense shrub very easily and is excellent as a pot plant, or try growing it as a beautiful miniature or quarter standard. Half hardy; Zones 9–10. Dyos, UK, 1984.

'Estelle Marie'

'Frank Saunders'

'Gay Fandango'

'Gay Fandango'

With its lax bushy habit, this fuchsia responds well to different ways of training. The flowers are medium to large doubles with a rosy-carmine tube, large rosy-carmine sepals and a long rosy-magenta corolla with the petals in two tiers. The mid-green foliage is medium to large in size and a lovely foil for the flowers. The large flower size may necessitate some support when training it as a pot plant. This cultivar is recommended for growing half or full standards. Half hardy; Zones 9–10. Nelson, USA, 1951.

'Gay Spinner'

The strong, vigorous and upright growth of this fuchsia creates a good pot plant if given plenty of early pinching to encourage branching. It is easy to train as a half or full standard as the stem will quickly grow to the necessary length. The flowers are medium to large semi-doubles with a pink tube, large pink sepals and an imperial purple corolla, with pink at the base at of the petals and extra petaloids inside. Raised by John Lockyer and released by his father Stuart. Half hardy; Zones 9–10. Lockyer, UK, 1978.

'Gordon Thorley'

This is a strong, upright and self-branching fuchsia with medium-sized single flowers with a pale rose-pink tube, pale rose-pink sepals held horizontally and a white corolla with petals edged and veined with rose. The plant is very floriferous, with mid- to dark green foliage contrasting beautifully with the flowers. It makes an excellent pot plant, and is very good for use in the border. This cultivar was hybridized from 'Cloverdale Pearl' and 'Santa Barbara'. Half hardy; Zones 9–10. Roe, UK, 1987.

'Happy Wedding Day'

This Australian cultivar has large double flowers featuring a white tube, white sepals with rose-bengal colouring near the tube and on the sepal edges and a tight white corolla. The foliage is mid-green with serrated edges and the growth is strong and upright, but made lax by the number and weight of the flowers, so it is best to add some canes as supports when growing it in a pot. It will rapidly make a spectacular plant. Half hardy; Zones 9–10. Richardson, Australia, 1985.

'Heidi Ann'

This cultivar is a bushy upright-growing plant, which will make a very good specimen pot plant or quarter standard

'Gay Spinner'

'Happy Wedding Day'

for the patio or garden. It has medium-sized double flowers with a carmine-red tube and sepals, and a lilac-veined cerise corolla with a double skirt of petals and petaloids, which are paler at the base. The growth is self-branching, with small dark green leaves with a red central vein. Both of this plant's parents, 'Tennessee Waltz' and 'General Monk', are hardy, and this cultivar inherits those characteristics, so it is a good choice for a permanent planting in the garden. Hardy; Zone 7. Growth 40cm (16in). Smith, UK, 1969.

'Herzilein'

This German cultivar is a bushy upright plant, whose name translates as 'Little Heart'. It has small single flowers with a long light orange-red tube and short light orange-red sepals that hang downwards, partially covering the dark red corolla. It is very free-flowering with medium-sized light to mid-green foliage. The plant is quite tolerant of full sun and looks good on its own in a pot or a patio container. Equally, it is very suitable for mixing with other plants in larger containers where it fills the gaps excellently. Half hardy; Zones 9–10. Strümper, Germany, 1989.

'Igloo Maid'

'Hessett Festival'

This is an upright and self-branching cultivar with very large double flowers, and grows to an impressive pot plant. The flowers have a short white tube, long white recurving sepals and a full lavender-blue corolla with white streaks. The medium-sized mid-green leaves have a fine serration around the edges. The plant makes a good half or full standard. Half hardy; Zones 9–10. Goulding, UK, 1985.

'Hidcote Beauty'

This cultivar, found by a British Fuchsia Society member growing at Hidcote Manor in Gloucestershire, England, has an abundance of medium-sized single flowers with a long waxy cream tube, waxy cream sepals tipped green and a pale salmon-orange corolla with pink shading. The foliage is medium to large and light green, and the growth upright and slightly lax. It makes an excellent specimen plant, a nice half standard and is also well worth using as a summer bedder. It is on the American Fuchsia Society's list of gall mite-resistant plants. Half hardy; Zones 9–10. Introducer Webb, UK, 1949.

'Hot Coals'

When first introduced, this fuchsia caused a stir because of its unusual flower colouring, aptly described by its name. The medium-sized single flowers have a dark red tube, dark scarlet-red semi-reflexed sepals and a dark aubergine corolla. The growth is upright, short-jointed and self-branching with mid- to dark green foliage. It forms a lovely pot plant with a minimum of effort. Half hardy; Zones 9–10. Carless, UK, 1993.

'Igloo Maid'

This is an upright-growing cultivar with medium to large double flowers with a white tube, white sepals tipped green and a full white corolla with a hint of pink. The medium-sized leaves are yellowish-green.

'Hidcote Beauty'

It makes a very impressive pot plant, and is often described as one of the best white doubles. Half hardy; Zones 9–10. Holmes, UK, 1972.

'Impudence'

This US cultivar is a naturally upright bush and makes a superb pot plant. The medium-sized single flowers have a light red tube, long light red sepals that are fully reflexed around the tube and a white corolla veined with rose in which the four petals are almost flat when fully open. The mid-green leaves complement the flower shape and colour. The upright habit makes the plant a good one to train as an espalier or fan. Half hardy; Zones 9–10. Schnabel, USA, 1957.

'Ivana van Amsterdam'

This is a cultivar with parentage from 'Pink Fantasia', in this case crossed with 'Lambada'. It shows some of the 'Pink Fantasia' characteristics, with its medium-sized single flower held erect with a greenish-white tube, pale rose sepals with green tips and a blue corolla which opens tight, then flares, maturing to pale mauve. It has a very bushy natural growth habit and is very free-flowering, so it will make a nice pot plant or smaller standard. Half hardy; Zones 9–10. van der Putten, Netherlands, 2002.

'Impudence'

'Jenny May'

'Jomam'

'Jenny May'

This is a very vigorous, strong-growing, self-branching upright with a slightly lax habit. It has medium to large single flowers with a creamy-pink tube, long creamy-pink sepals and a violet corolla with pink splashes. The foliage is medium to large in size and mid-green in colour, and the growth is especially suited to bush-training as a pot plant. Half hardy; Zones 9–10. Bush, UK, 1998.

'Jessica Reynolds'

This is a more recent cultivar with a very good upright, short-jointed and self-branching habit. The plentiful medium-sized single flowers have a white tube, white sepals flushed aubergine and a compact aubergine corolla. The medium-sized mid-green leaves perfectly complement the flower colours. It is quite strong-growing, so it makes an excellent pot plant and quarter or half standard. Half hardy; Zones 9–10. Reynolds, UK, 2000.

'Joan Goy'

The erect flowers of this fuchsia create a very fetching pot plant, but it needs hard pinching early on. The flowers are medium-sized singles with a white-pink tube and sepals, and a lilac-pink flared corolla with pale patches at the petal base. The buds grow in clusters at the end of the stems

and the flowers appear to grow as they mature, but the gradual flaring of the corolla probably causes this effect. The small to medium-sized foliage is dark green. It is a delightful cultivar that is well worth growing. Half hardy; Zones 9–10. Webb, UK, 1989.

'Joel'

This is an upright cultivar that is quite self-branching, but benefits from extra pinching early on. The flowers are pretty, medium-sized singles held semi-erect, and have a white tube, white reflexed sepals with a faint pink blush and an exquisite pale violet-blue corolla that flares beautifully.

It is not the strongest growing cultivar but is well worth trying for the flowers and their contrast with the small to medium-sized mid- to dark green leaves. It is excellent when grown as a smallish pot plant or small standard. Half hardy; Zones 9–10. Humphries, UK, 1993.

'Jomam'

This upright, short-jointed bushy fuchsia makes a superb, really eye-catching pot plant. The flowers are medium-sized singles with a rose-pink tube, quite large rose-pink sepals that tend to twist slightly and a quarter-flared pale blue-violet corolla that matures to light violet-pink. The strong stems produce vigorous growth with dark yellowish-green leaves, and it quickly becomes a large plant. Take care to keep the roots cool because it dislikes being overheated. Half hardy; Zones 9–10. Hall, UK, 1984.

'Kath van Hanegem'

This small-growing cultivar is very pretty and suitable for growing as a smaller pot plant or miniature standard. It is named after an enthusiastic fuchsia grower living in the east of England and married to a Dutchman. The small but exquisite single flowers have a dark red tube, red sepals and an aubergine corolla. The mid-green leaves contrast well with the flowers. It is also suitable for a rockery in warm areas. Frost hardy; Zones 7–8. Carless, UK, 1998.

'Kath van Hanegem'

'Katie Susan'

'London 2000'

'Katie Susan'

This quite new cultivar is a very vigorous grower. It is short-jointed, upright and bushy, and quickly makes an excellent pot plant. The flowers are medium-sized singles with a rose tube and sepals, and a flared cyclamen-purple corolla with lighter patches near the base of the petals. The foliage is medium-sized and attractive light green. Unlike most fuchsias, it tends to produce just one flower from each leaf axil, but it makes up for that with the number of branches and hence the number of flowers. Half hardy; Zones 9–10. Waving, UK, 2004.

'Lady Isobel Barnett'

'Kobold'

This bushy fuchsia has small to medium-sized semi-erect single flowers with a red tube and sepals, and a bell-shaped violet-blue corolla. When grown as a pot plant or standard, the flower colour is really eye-catching, and it continues flowering over a long period. The upright, short-jointed growth carries small to medium-sized mid-green leaves. Half hardy; Zones 9–10. Götz, Germany, 1990.

'Lady Isobel Barnett'

This is one of the most floriferous cultivars, with as many as four flowers from each leaf node. The single flowers are small to medium-sized with a rosy-red tube and sepals, and a rose-purple corolla with darker edges on the petals. The growth is upright, self-branching and bushy with medium-sized mid-green foliage. It is easy to grow as a specimen pot plant or for summer bedding. Half hardy; Zones 9–10. Gadsby, UK, 1968.

'Lambada'

This is a compact, pretty cultivar which is very useful for small pots. It has small single flowers with a pale pink tube and sepals and a mallow-purple flared corolla with white patches at the petal base. The growth is upright and compact with small

mid-green foliage. It has a tremendous number of flowers, making it a great pot plant or small standard. It is also excellent for use in mixed plantings. Half hardy; Zones 9–10. Götz, Germany, 1989.

'Lilac Lustre'

This is an attractive cultivar that has beautifully shaped flowers and fat, round buds that hang in the bright mid-green foliage. The freely produced medium-sized double flowers have a rose-red tube and sepals, and a powder-blue corolla with ruffled petals. It makes an excellent pot plant, but prefers to grow in a shady position. Half hardy; Zones 9–10. Munkner, USA, 1961.

'London 2000'

This is a good, strong and vigorous upright cultivar, excellent as a pot plant or a small to medium standard. The flowers are medium-sized singles with a white tube blushed pink, white sepals flushed pink and a cyclamen-purple corolla with cerise areas at the base of the petals. The corolla fades to cerise as the flower matures. The medium-sized mid-green leaves provide an excellent backdrop for the abundant flowers, and it can also be trained into other shapes, such as a fan. Half hardy; Zones 9–10. Weston, UK, 2000.

'Marcus Graham'

'Mrs Susan Brookfield'

'Marcus Graham'

An introduction from Annabelle Stubbs, this cultivar never fails to make an impact. The growth is upright, quite vigorous and self-branching, and needs to be well hardened to support the large double flowers, which have a thin white to flesh-pink tube, long broad dusky pink sepals and a fully flared salmon-pink full corolla with orange streaks on the petals. The foliage is quite large and mid-green. This fuchsia can be grown as a specimen bush or standard as well as a pot plant. Half hardy; Zones 9–10. Stubbs, USA, 1985.

'Margaret Roe'

This is a free-flowering cultivar that has vigorous and upright growth. The medium-sized single flowers are held upright and have a short rosy-red tube and sepals, and a violet-purple corolla. The medium-sized foliage is dull mid-green and the strong growth benefits from early pinching. It is excellent as a pot plant, in a patio container or planted permanently in the garden. Hardy; Zone 7. Growth 75cm (30in). Gadsby, UK, 1968.

'Maria Landy'

With its vigorous, upright, self-branching growth, this makes an excellent compact specimen plant. The prolific flowers are semi-erect small singles with a pale pink tube, recurving pink sepals and a pale

violet corolla. The foliage is small and dark green, a perfect foil for the beautiful flowers. It can be trained as a small standard, or used in mixed planting or for summer bedding. Half hardy; Zones 9–10. Wilkinson, UK, 1991.

'Micky Goult'

Upright and free-flowering, this has clusters of small, single, semi-erect flowers with a short pale pink tube, horizontal pale pink sepals tipped green and a short mallow-purple corolla. The foliage is light to mid-green, and quite large for the flower

'Maria Landy'

size. Its upright growth needs heavy early pinching to create a bushy shape, but if left to grow naturally it flowers early and over a long period. Half hardy; Zones 9–10. Roe, UK, 1986.

'Mrs Susan Brookfield'

This is an attractive upright with medium-sized double flowers with a dark rose tube, reflexed dark rose sepals and a full mauve corolla with attractive pink and rose splashes. The medium-sized bright pale to mid-green foliage provides an excellent foil to the flowers. The growth is strongly upright with reasonable self-branching, but it is helped by early pinching. The best colours with the brightest petal splashes are obtained when grown outside in part direct sun, part shade, where it makes an excellent pot plant or half standard. Half hardy; Zones 9–10. Rimmer, UK, 1991.

'Nico van Suchtelen'

This Dutch cultivar has strong upright self-branching growth with large mid-green leaves. The flowers are long medium-sized singles, almost Triphylla-like with a long carmine pink tube, streaked with a darker shade, light carmine pink sepals held downwards and a short carmine corolla, which is deep carmine pink at the base. It makes an unusual large pot plant and thrives in full sun. Half hardy; Zones 9–10. Benders, Netherlands, 1986.

'Northern Dancer'

'Orange Flare'

'Northern Dancer'

The small double flowers of this fuchsia have a red tube, red sepals with a white base and green tips, and a light purple corolla with a pink flush. With upright and self-branching growth, it makes a very pretty small pot plant. Half hardy; Zones 9–10. Wilkinson, UK, 2000.

'Northway'

This produces small single flowers held semi-erect with a pale pink tube, pale pink sepals held just below the horizontal and a bright cherry-red corolla. The foliage is light to mid-green and contrasts well with the flower colours. With upright self-branching growth, it makes a striking pot plant. Half hardy; Zones 9–10. Golics, UK, 1976.

'Northumbrian Pipes'

This cultivar is something different, with unusual flower colours and buds. It has Triphylla-type flowers held on part terminal and part axial flowering growth. They are medium-sized singles with a long china-rose tube, short china-rose sepals tipped green and a light lavender-pink corolla. The growing buds are also an attractive, unusual colour, with the ovary and half of the tube almost aubergine, and the remainder green. The lax bushy upright growth has long mid- to dark green leaves, which are lighter underneath. It does well in a pot or small patio container. Half hardy; Zones 9–10. de Graaff, Netherlands, 1983.

'Onna'

Very floriferous, this fuchsia is upright and self-branching with Triphylla-shaped flowers, but they emerge from the leaf axils and not the end of the stems. The medium-sized single flowers have a long orange tube, short orange sepals held down over the corolla with recurving tips,

'Onna'

and a crimson corolla. The largish leaves are mid-green and lighter underneath with green stems. It makes a nice pot or patio container plant. Half hardy; Zones 9–10. Bögemann, Germany, 1987.

'Orange Flare'

This cultivar is perhaps one of the best orange-flowered fuchsias, apart from those in the Triphylla Group. It has an early-flowering habit, and is a plant that will be quite happy in full sun, although the colours do benefit from slight shading. The flowers are medium-sized singles with a short thick orange-salmon tube, orange-salmon sepals and an orange corolla, lighter at the petal base and darker on the petal edges. The growth is upright and bushy with medium-sized mid-green foliage. It makes a good pot plant or standard. Half hardy; Zones 9–10. Handley, UK, 1986.

'Our Darling'

This is a strong upright-growing cultivar that self-branches very well and is suitable for training as a bush, a shrub or a standard. The medium-sized single flowers have a short deep rose tube, reflexed deep rose sepals and a flared violet-blue corolla veined with rose and with lighter patches at the petal base. It is very floriferous with medium to large mid-green leaves, and makes a beautiful specimen plant in a pot. Half hardy; Zones 9–10. Hall, UK, 1984.

'Pabbe's Kirrevaalk'

'Phenomenal'

'Pabbe's Kirrevaalk'

This Dutch cultivar has bushy upright growth with small single flowers, held semi-erect, with a short dark reddish-purple tube, reddish-purple sepals held horizontally and a flared saucer-shaped corolla opening dark purple, maturing to reddish-purple. The small mid-green foliage provides a good foil to the copious amounts of flowers. It is easy to grow as a pot plant or smaller standard. Half hardy; Zones 9–10. Koerts, Netherlands, 2004.

'Patio Princess'

This is a vigorous and spreading self-branching bush which is easy to grow and, as its name suggests, will make an excellent specimen plant for the patio. It flowers early in the season with small to medium double flowers with a neyron-rose tube, neyron-rose three-quarters recurving sepals, and a flared white corolla veined with red. The foliage is small to medium, mid-green with a red vein in the leaf. It does tend to throw a number of semi-double flowers as well, but the sheer quantity of flowers produced will compensate for this. Half hardy; Zones 9–10. Sinton, UK, 1988.

'Phenomenal'

This fuchsia is certainly a striking sight today, but it must have been really spectacular when it was first released in the middle of the 19th century. It has large double flowers with a thin scarlet tube, broad scarlet sepals and a lovely indigo-blue corolla with cerise veining on the petals, which are paler at the base. The mid-green foliage is largish and serrated, and the flowers are freely produced for their size. The branches may need some staking to support the weight of the flowers. Half hardy; Zones 9–10. Lemoine, France, 1869.

'Plumb Bob'

The flowers of this fuchsia are large doubles with an ivory tube flushed pink, ivory sepals with a pink flush and a red corolla with mauve tones, and they are quite numerous for their size. The medium-sized foliage is mid- to dark green and a perfect backdrop to the flowers. Use this vigorous sturdy upright as a specimen pot plant, a standard or in summer bedding. Half hardy; Zones 9–10. Goulding, UK, 1974.

'President Leo Boullemier'

This is a vigorous upright cultivar that will make a good specimen pot plant or a standard, and also grows well as a summer bedding plant. The flowers are medium-sized singles with a square white tube streaked magenta, white recurving sepals and a bell-shaped magenta corolla. The foliage is medium-sized and dark green in colour. The plant is a cross between 'Joy Patmore' and 'Cloverdale Pearl'. Half hardy; Zones 9–10. Burns, UK, 1983.

'Queen Mary'

This old cultivar, one of a pair of seedlings named after the then reigning British monarchs, is a vigorous upright bush. It has large single flowers, which are quite abundant for their size, with a pale pink tube, long pink sepals tipped greenish-white and a rose corolla that matures to mauve-purple. The largish mid-green leaves help create an impressive pot plant that can easily be trained into a medium to large standard. Half hardy; Zones 9–10. Howlett, UK, 1911.

'President Leo Boullemier'

'Query'

'Ratatouille'

'Query'

This very old cultivar, still popular, has a small single flower with a pale pink tube, pale pink sepals with green tips and a purple corolla veined pink that matures to magenta. The growth is upright and self-branching with rather small light to mid-green leaves, and it makes a nice pot plant. This cultivar is very similar to 'Chillerton Beauty', introduced by the same hybridizer in the same year, and some believe it may be the same plant. Hardy; Zones 6–7. Growth 60cm (24in). Bass, UK, 1848.

'Ratatouille'

This Dutch cultivar has an unusual parentage, a result from crossing a fuchsia species with a showy US double. This created the small to medium-sized double flowers with an ivory-white tube, ivory-white sepals blushed lilac underneath and a pale aubergine corolla with white stripes. The growth is upright and slightly lax with medium-sized, bright mid-green foliage, and it makes an excellent pot plant. Half hardy; Zones 9–10. de Graaff, Netherlands, 1988.

'Robert Lutters'

This is a vigorous upright bush that is excellent as a pot plant or trained as a standard. The plentiful flowers are medium-sized singles with a white tube blushed rose, rose sepals held horizontally

and slightly twisted, and a quarter flared bengal-red corolla with a classic bell shape. The medium-sized light to mid-green leaves complement the flowers very well. Half hardy; Zones 9–10. Beije, Netherlands, 1989.

'Rocket Fire'

This is a vigorous upright bush cultivar with unusual double flowers that are medium in size with a magenta tube, dark rose sepals and a corolla with purple pleated outer petals and dark pink inner petals. The foliage is medium to large and mid-green, and provides a nice

background to the flowers. This fuchsia makes a good pot plant. Half hardy; Zones 9–10. Garrett, USA, 1989.

'Rolla'

This old French cultivar grows excellently as a bush, vigorous and upright. It was one of the 50 cultivars sent to the USA in 1930 and is probably in the parentage of many of the large US double fuchsias. The flowers are large doubles with a short pale pink tube, pale pink sepals fully reflexed over the tube and a full pure white corolla with pink tinges at the petal base. The medium-sized mid-green foliage helps make it an attractive pot plant, and it can be trained into large structures. Half hardy; Zones 9–10. Lemoine, France, 1913.

'Roy Walker'

This cultivar is one of the better white doubles, staying white even in the sun. The growth is upright and self-branching with medium-sized mid-green foliage; it needs to be grown hard (outdoors as much as possible) to make the wood strong enough to support the flowers. The flower is a medium to large double with a white tube flushed pink, white-veined red sepals and a flared white corolla. This fuchsia takes a long time from final pinching to flowering, typically 12 to 14 weeks. It will make a striking specimen plant or half standard. Half hardy; Zones 9–10. Fuchsia-La, USA, 1975.

'Roy Walker'

'Sarah Eliza'

'Sarah Eliza'

There is some confusion over the growth habit of this cultivar. It is often listed as a trailing fuchsia, but it has growth that is more bush-like, and it is just the weight of the flowers that makes the branches hang downward. The flower is a medium to large double with a white tube, white sepals flushed pale pink and a full white corolla flushed pink. Like most white fuchsias, the flower becomes pinker in the sun, especially the sepals. The growth is upright and spreading with light green leaves, and it is quite floriferous, making it ideal as a pot plant or in the centre of a mixed basket or container. Half hardy; Zones 9–10. Clements, UK, 1992.

'Satellite'

This has rather unusual medium to large double flowers with a greenish-white tube, white sepals with green tips and a dark red corolla streaked white. The strongly upright growth has medium-sized mid-green foliage and the flowers look superb together with it, standing out in the sunshine. It makes a very striking pot plant for the terrace or patio. Take care not to overwater it as it is prone to botrytis. Half hardy; Zones 9–10. Kennett, USA, 1965.

'Silver Dawn'

This is a strong upright bushy cultivar with medium-sized mid-green foliage, and is excellent for growing as a pot plant or a half standard. The medium-sized double flowers have a long white tube, broad white sepals tipped green and a beautiful aster-violet corolla. Half hardy; Zones 9–10. Bellamy, UK, 1983.

'Snowfire'

This is an introduction from Annabelle Stubbs. A very striking fuchsia, it will make an excellent pot plant, or is useful for growing in mixed containers. The flower is a large double with a pink tube, wide white sepals and a bright coral corolla with white patches, which are larger on the outer petals. The foliage is medium to large in size and dark green in colour. This fuchsia always attracts people's attention. Half hardy; Zones 9–10. Stubbs, USA, 1978.

'Sunray'

This is one of the best of the variegated-leaf cultivars. It forms a slow-growing bush, with the best leaf colours developed in the sun or bright conditions. Although grown more for its foliage than the flowers, they are not unattractive, being small to medium-sized singles with a cerise tube, cerise sepals and a rosy-purple corolla. The foliage is medium-sized and has yellow, green and red colours in the leaf. This fuchsia will form an attractive smaller pot plant or blend well in a mixed container. An alternative plant to consider is 'Tom West', which is a little faster growing, but the leaf colours are not quite as good. Half hardy; Zones 9–10. Rudd, UK, 1872.

'Symphony'

This beautiful cultivar is very tall and graceful, with medium-sized single flowers with a pale phlox-pink tube, slightly reflexed pale phlox-pink sepals and a cobalt-violet corolla. The mid-green foliage with slightly lighter yellow-green new growth helps make an attractive, striking pot plant. Quite fast growing, it will make a shrub quickly. It prefers a shady position. This is a plant that deserves to be more widely grown than it is. Half hardy; Zones 9–10. Neiderholzer, USA, 1944.

'Snowfire'

'Symphony'

'Thamar'

'Taddle'

A vigorous free-flowering upright self-branching cultivar with medium-sized light green foliage, this fuchsia can be trained as a bush with the minimum of effort. The flowers are medium-sized singles with a short deep rose-pink tube, fully reflexed rose-pink sepals and a waxy white-veined pink corolla. Half hardy; Zones 9–10. Gubler, UK, 1974.

'Tamar Isobel'

This fuchsia has vigorous upright and bushy growth with small to medium-sized mid-green leaves. The medium-sized single flowers have a white tube striped with pink, fully recurved white sepals with a slight pink blush and a reddish-purple corolla with pink streaks. It makes an excellent pot plant with minimal effort, and is easy to grow as a standard, best as a half standard. This was one of the last introductions from the hybridizer before his death that same year. Half hardy; Zones 9–10. Mitchinson, UK, 1988.

'Tangerine'

This US cultivar is a *F. cordifolia* seedling with medium-sized single flowers with a long, flesh-pink tube, flesh-pink sepals tipped green and a flared orange corolla with overlapping petals maturing to rose. The growth habit is upright and bushy with mid-green leaves, and it makes an attractive spreading pot plant. Half hardy; Zones 9–10. Tiret, USA, 1949.

'Thamar'

This eye-catching cultivar is rather unusual, with its upright growth and many flowers held erect like little pansies. The flowers are small singles with a white tube, white cupped sepals with a faint pink blush and a pale blue corolla with white patches at the base. The foliage is medium-sized and dark green. It is a very floriferous plant, but the growth is not self-branching, so it benefits from early pinching. It stays in flower for a long time and makes a good specimen pot plant, container plant or summer bedder. This cultivar is well worth growing for its impact. Half hardy; Zones 9–10. Springer, Germany, 1986.

'Ting a Ling'

This is an upright bushy cultivar, which is excellent grown as a shrub pot plant or as a quarter or half standard. It has medium-sized single flowers with a white tube, three-quarters recurved white sepals and a white bell-shaped, flared corolla. The medium-sized foliage is mid-green and it grows well but, like many whites, can be prone to botrytis. Half hardy; Zones 9–10. Schnabel and Paskesen, USA, 1959.

'Ting a Ling'

'Twinny'

This relative newcomer is already very popular, making an impressive pot plant or a smaller standard up to half standard size. The flowers are small to medium-sized singles with a red tube, pink-red sepals and white corolla with red veining. The growth is upright, self-branching, very bushy and floriferous, with small mid- to dark green leaves. It dislikes heat, so when grown in a pot, terracotta is best, and the pot should be shaded. Half hardy; Zones 9–10. Gordon, UK, 1999.

'Twinny'

'Upward Look'

'Upward Look'
This vigorous upright bushy cultivar has medium-sized erect single flowers with a carmine tube, carmine sepals with green tips and a pale purple corolla. This was the first notable fuchsia with erect flowers released since 'Bon Accord' in 1861. It has dull mid-green foliage and grows well in full sun, and makes an excellent specimen pot plant, standard and summer bedder. Half hardy; Zones 9–10. Gadsby, UK, 1968.

'Uranus'
This German cultivar has medium-sized single flowers with a short fat red tube, long reflexed red sepals and a dark purple corolla. Upright growing and bushy with mid- to dark green foliage, it is easy to train to a bush or shrub pot plant or even as a standard. Half hardy; Zones 9–10. Strümper, Germany, 1986.

'Vincent van Gogh'
This Dutch cultivar, named after the famous artist, has strong upright bushy growth covered by bright mid-green foliage. The flowers are small to medium-sized singles with a long pink tube, pale pink sepals with green tips that hang down and a pale lilac-pink corolla that is slightly flared. It is a good plant for training as a bush or shrub in a pot. Half hardy; Zones 9–10. van der Post, Netherlands, 1984.

'Violet Bassett-Burr'
The flowers of this fuchsia are beautiful and highly unusual, sure to create a striking impression. They are large doubles with a greenish-white and pink tube, almost fully recurved white sepals with green tips and pink at the base, and a very full pale lilac corolla. The growth is upright

'Voodoo'

and bushy, and the foliage dark green. It is at its best grown as a specimen pot plant or a full or half standard. This fuchsia is one that will turn heads, and is well worth growing. Half hardy; Zones 9–10. Holmes, UK, 1972.

'Vobeglo'
This compact, low-growing fuchsia has small erect single flowers with a pink tube, rose-red sepals and a lilac-purple corolla. The growth is bushy but not very vigorous, with small to medium-sized mid-green foliage. It will happily make a small pot plant, a small standard, or can be used in a rockery. Half hardy; Zones 9–10. de Groot, Netherlands, 1974.

'Voodoo'
This has spectacular large double flowers with a dark red tube, long dark red sepals and a very full dark purple-violet corolla with some red splashes at the base of the petals. The growth is vigorous, bushy and upright, with medium to large mid-green foliage. Grow outside as much as possible to harden the wood so that it can support the large flowers, or use stakes. It is an excellent cultivar to grow as a specimen plant for a large pot. Half hardy; Zones 9–10. Tiret, USA, 1953.

'Vobeglo'

'White Joy'

'White Joy'

This strong-growing cultivar with an upright, bushy habit is very easy to grow as a pot plant or a quarter or half standard. The flowers are medium-sized singles with a short white tube with a pink blush, white recurving sepals with a pink blush and a flared bell-shaped white corolla. The foliage is medium-sized and light to mid-green. Half hardy; Zones 9–10. Burns, UK, 1980.

'Wilson's Sugar Pink'

This vigorous cultivar is bush-like but can tend to become a little lax. Growing it in full sun strengthens the wood and helps keep it upright. The flowers are produced in great abundance. They are small singles with a white tube shading to pink, pale pink sepals and a silver-pink corolla. The small to medium-sized leaves are an attractive shade of light green. Half hardy; Zones 9–10. Wilson, UK, 1979.

'Wingrove's Mammoth'

This has very large double flowers with a short turkey-red tube, long turkey-red sepals and a very full white corolla veined and splashed with carmine. It is upright and bushy but the heavy flowers drag the branches down, so some support and staking may be necessary. The medium-sized foliage is mid-green. Half hardy; Zones 9–10. Wingrove, UK, 1986.

'Woodnook'

This upright and bushy cultivar has attractive medium-sized double flowers with a white tube striped with carmine, white sepals flushed carmine and tipped with green and a pale violet-purple full corolla with rose-bengal splashes. The medium-sized foliage is mid-green in colour and the profuse flowers stand out beautifully. This vigorous growing fuchsia makes a superb pot plant and is excellent grown as a half standard. Half hardy; Zones 9–10. Pacey, UK, 1987.

'Yolanda Franck'

This Dutch cultivar has medium-sized single flowers with a thick light rose tube, light rose sepals tipped green hanging down and a pale orange-red corolla. The strong upright growth is self-branching with medium-sized mid-green leaves. Fairly free-flowering, it makes a nice pot plant and is happy in full sun. Half hardy; Zones 9–10. Franck, Netherlands, 1988.

'Zwarte Snor'

This attractive Dutch cultivar has medium-sized single to semi-double flowers with a slightly barrel-shaped cardinal-red tube, cardinal-red sepals hanging down and a purple-aubergine corolla with red at the base of the petals. The growth is upright, self-branching and slightly lax, with medium-sized mid-green foliage, which contrasts well with the abundantly produced flowers. It does best in a shady position, and is easy to grow to a good-sized pot plant, trained as a shrub. Half hardy; Zones 9–10. Weeda, Netherlands, 1990.

'Wilson's Sugar Pink'

'Wingrove's Mammoth'

Hardy fuchsias

When planted correctly outside, hardy fuchsias should survive winter temperatures down to -23°C (-10°F). The heights stated are typically achieved with winter temperatures between -18 and -12°C (0 to 10°F), when the fuchsias are planted in a sunny position.

'Abbé Farges'

This pretty cultivar has small semi-double flowers with a light cerise tube, light cerise reflexed sepals and a lilac-blue corolla with slightly scalloped petal edges. The growth is rather wiry and slightly brittle, but it is surprisingly vigorous and free-flowering. Try growing it as a quarter standard, which will be completely covered in flowers. It is a good garden hardy that is ideal for the middle or front of the hardy border. Hardy; Zone 6. Growth 45–60cm (18–24in). Lemoine, France, 1901.

'Achievement'

This vigorous old cultivar is easy to grow, making it a good choice for beginners. It has large single flowers with a short red tube, long red sepals and a corolla that opens purple and fades to reddish-purple on maturity. The foliage is yellowish-green with a distinct red midrib. It is sometimes confused with 'Charming' but has longer, narrower, less reflexed sepals. It is good in the middle of the hardy border or can be grown as a pot plant. Hardy; Zone 6. Growth 55cm (22in). Melville, UK, 1866.

'Alice Hoffman'

One of the smaller-growing hardy fuchsias, this cultivar has small semi-double flowers with tube and sepals both coloured rose, and a white, veined rose corolla. The growth is wiry, spreading and upright, and the foliage is small and bronze-green. A compact growing bush, it does well at the front of the hardy border and is useful in the rockery. It will also make an effective small standard. This cultivar has an RHS Award of Garden Merit, awarded in 2002. Hardy; Zones 7–8. Growth 45cm (18in). Kiese, Germany, 1911.

'Army Nurse'

This is a strong upright bush with medium-sized semi-double flared flowers with a short red tube, red sepals and a mauve-blue corolla, pink blushed at the petal base. It has vigorous growth with light to mid-green foliage, making a fair-sized plant in one season. Grow it as a pot plant, or plant it out as a summer bedder. It received an RHS Award of Garden Merit in 1993. Hardy; Zone 7. Growth 1m (3ft). Hodges, USA, 1947.

'Baby Blue Eyes'

'Baby Blue Eyes'

This cultivar has upright and strong bushy growth with small single flowers. The flowers have red sepals and tube and a dark lavender corolla, and the foliage is medium-sized and dark green in colour. It is very floriferous, and grows well in the middle of a hardy bed where it forms a compact bushy shrub. This cultivar has an RHS Award of Garden Merit, awarded in 2005. Hardy; Zones 6–7. Growth 1m (3ft). Plummer, USA, 1952.

'Bashful'

This small upright, self-branching bushy cultivar has small double flowers with a deep pink tube and sepals and a white corolla with red veining. Raised and bred in the Scilly Isles, it is one of the Seven Dwarfs series of cultivars and has compact growth with small dark green foliage, making it ideal for a rockery or to the front of the hardy border. Although listed as a hardy, it is probably better classified as a marginal hardy. Hardy; Zones 7–8. Growth 30cm (12in). Tabraham, UK, 1974.

'Alice Hoffman'

'Army Nurse'

'Beacon'

This old hardy cultivar has quite stiff upright growth and medium-sized single flowers with a deep pink tube and sepals, and a mauvish-pink flared corolla. The foliage is a darkish green with wavy serrated edges. It is a very reliable plant, which you can also train as a standard. Older specimens have very unusual bark on the wood, which becomes flaky and peels off. There is a sport from 'Beacon' called 'Beacon Rosa', where the flowers are the same shape but self-pink in colour. Hardy; Zone 7. Growth 60cm (2ft). Bull, UK, 1871.

'Brilliant'

This reliable old hardy has strong upright, vigorous open growth and mid- to dark green foliage. The medium-sized single or semi-double flowers have a long scarlet tube, slightly reflexed scarlet sepals and a violet-magenta corolla with red veining on the petals. It is a good hardy for the middle to rear of any hardy scheme, but is also suitable as a summer bedder or trained as a standard. Hardy; Zone 7. Growth 70cm (28in). Bull, UK, 1865.

'Caledonia'

This has quite vigorous, spreading upright growth and medium-green foliage. The single flowers are rather unusual for a

'Brilliant'

hardy fuchsia, having long cerise tubes, cerise sepals that hang down and a crimson corolla. It is a good candidate to grow in the mid-position in the hardy border and also makes an attractive low hedge. Hardy; Zones 6–7. Growth 65cm (26in). Lemoine, France, 1899.

'Charming'

This is an easily grown hardy cultivar, upright and vigorous with medium-sized single flowers with a carmine tube, nicely reflexed reddish-cerise sepals and a rose-purple corolla. The flower is the classic

fuchsia shape and sits well against the medium-sized yellowish-green foliage. It makes a successful standard. It is sometimes confused with 'Drame', but has longer flowers and more upright growth. It received an RHS Award of Merit in 1929. Hardy; Zones 6–7. Growth 70cm (27in). Lye, UK, 1895.

'Chillerton Beauty'

Strong and reliable, this fuchsia has upright bushy growth and a profusion of small single flowers. The white tube is blushed pink and the horizontal sepals are the same colour, becoming pinker with more sun. The red-veined mauvish-violet corolla fades as the flower ages. It makes a good medium-sized hedge. Some believe it to be identical to 'Query'. Hardy; Zones 6–7. Growth 65cm (26in). Bass, UK, 1847.

'Cliff's Hardy'

This upright bushy cultivar has single medium-sized semi-erect flowers with a light crimson tube, light crimson sepals tipped green and a violet corolla. The flowers sit nicely held off the small mid- to dark green leaves. It is a vigorous grower, ideal for a fuchsia hedge. Do not overfeed, because it will make growth at the expense of flowers. Hardy; Zones 6–7. Growth 55cm (22in). Gadsby, UK, 1966.

'Caledonia'

'Charming'

'David'

'David'

A seedling from 'Pumila' and 'Venus Victrix', this has small leaves and flowers. It inherits many of the former's characteristics, carrying profuse single flowers with a cerise tube and sepals, and a rich purple corolla. The growth is compact and upright with small dark green leaves, making it very useful in the rockery, at the front of the hardy border and as an edging plant. Hardy; Zones 6–7. Growth 45cm (18in). Wood, UK, 1937.

'Display'

This excellent old exhibition-class cultivar is a strong upright and bushy grower with serrated mid- to dark green foliage. It has medium single flowers with rose-pink tube and sepals, and a darker pink flared corolla. It is very easy to train and can be used for most forms of trained growth, including pyramids and standards. It is popular in Germany and the Netherlands. This is an ideal candidate for everyone's collection. Hardy; Zones 6–7. Growth 60cm (2ft). Smith, UK, 1881.

'Dollar Prinzessin' ('Dollar Princess'/'Princess Dollar')

Although still sold widely as 'Dollar Princess', research has shown that the original name of this fuchsia was 'Dollarprinzessin'. Attributed to Victor Lemoine and introduced in 1912, a year after his death, it now seems it was first introduced in Germany by Kroger in 1910. It is a cultivar which, when grown in the border, will make a mound covered in flowers. It has medium-sized double flowers with cerise tube and sepals and a rich purple full corolla, splashed red, with mid- to dark green foliage. It is one of the few double cultivars that can be treated as a hardy in cold areas, and will be in flower shortly after midsummer. It is at its best in the second or third year when grown as a pot plant, and also makes a good standard. Hardy; Zones 6–7. Growth 40cm (16in). Kroger, Germany, 1910.

'Empress of Prussia'

This old cultivar was thought to have been lost from cultivation, but a plant was discovered in an English garden in 1956, where it had been growing for more than 60 years. After propagation, Bernard Rawlings reintroduced it. It has medium to large single flowers with a scarlet tube and sepals, and a corolla of reddish-magenta petals with a paler patch near the base. It is very floriferous, throwing up to four flowers from each leaf axil, with strong upright growth. Hardy; Zones 6–7. Growth 90cm (3ft). Hoppe, UK, 1868.

'Display'

'Dollar Prinzessin'

'Enfant Prodigue' ('Prodigue'/'Prodigy')

This old cultivar has strong, vigorous upright growth, inherited from one of its parents, 'Riccartonii'. It has medium-sized semi-double – sometimes double – flowers with a deep red tube and sepals, and a deep blue corolla with red at the base of the petals. With its medium-sized, mid-green foliage, it is best towards the back of the hardy border where it will form a large plant. Hardy; Zones 6–7. Growth 90cm (3ft). Lemoine, France, 1887.

'Eva Boerg'

This cultivar is an unusual hardy, being quite lax and growing into a spreading bush. It is a good cultivar for use in hanging baskets, beds held back by a retaining wall and permanent planting in planters built into walls. The growth will soon spread over the wall and trail down it. The flesh-pink buds are very fat and round before opening into a medium-sized semi-double flower with a greenish-white tube, pinkish-white sepals and pinkish-purple corolla splashed pink at the base. The foliage is a light green, and the cultivar is often confused with the very similar 'Lena'. This fuchsia is easy to grow into a weeping standard because of its strong growth. Hardy; Zone 7. Growth 45cm (18in). Yorke, UK, 1943.

'Flash'

This hardy US cultivar is vigorous, bushy and upright in growth habit, with small, finely serrated light green foliage. It is quite floriferous, carrying small single flowers with a light-magenta tube and sepals, and a light-magenta corolla fading to red. It is quite a strong grower, well suited for use in the centre of the hardy border. Hardy; Zone 7. Growth 75cm (30in). Hazard and Hazard, USA, 1930.

'Foxgrove Wood'

This fairly recent cultivar has upright bushy growth and mid-green foliage. The pretty, small single flowers have a pink tube and sepals and blue corolla. This fuchsia can be grown in a hardy border, but in colder areas is best used as a summer bedder. Hardy; Zones 7–8. Growth 60cm (2ft). Stiff, UK, 1993.

'Frau Hilde Rademacher'

This is a beautiful fuchsia with rather lax, spreading growth. It is very floriferous for the size of the flowers, and has some resemblance to 'Dark Eyes'. The fat red buds open into medium to large double flowers with a short red tube, horizontal red sepals and a full, frilled, deep blue corolla. The foliage is dark green with red veining. It can be trained as a weeping half standard. Hardy; Zones 7–8. Growth 90cm (3ft). Rademacher, Germany, 1925.

'Garden News'

This is a good hardy double cultivar for the garden, with strong upright growth and mid-green foliage. The double flowers are medium to large with a pink tube and sepals and a full magenta corolla with ruffled petals. It is reliable and quite free-flowering for a double. Hardy; Zones 6–7. Growth 60cm (2ft). Handley, UK, 1978.

'Genii' ('Jeanne')

This is an excellent cultivar in all ways, and should be in everyone's garden. It is one of the few hardies originating from the USA. It was originally named 'Jeanne', but is now much more widely known as 'Genii'. It has beautiful small pale green foliage, which becomes lighter in the sun. It has single small to medium flowers with a cerise tube and sepals and a violet corolla. Because of its leaf colour, it seems to sparkle and stand out in the hardy border. You can also train it as a standard or grow it as a specimen plant in a large pot. Hardy; Zones 6–7. Growth 70cm (28in). Reiter, USA, 1951.

'Garden News'

'Gustaf Doré'

This old French cultivar is upright, bushy and self-branching with mid-green foliage. The flowers are medium-sized doubles with a deep pink tube, deep pink sepals and a creamy-white corolla, very full and fluffy, with attractive scalloped petal edges. This fuchsia is a good choice for the front of the border. Hardy; Zone 7. Growth 40cm (16in). Lemoine, France, 1880.

'Frau Hilde Rademacher'

'Genii'

'Happy'

This is one of the Seven Dwarfs series, a very attractive bush with compact, self-branching growth. It has small semi-erect single flowers with a red tube and sepals, and a deep purple-blue corolla turning magenta. The flowers resemble small stars twinkling on a small green mound of foliage. It is excellent as an edging plant or for use in the rockery, or the front of the hardy border and grown as a small pot. Hardy; Zone 8. Growth 40cm (16in). Tabraham, UK, 1974.

'Hawkshead'

This is a superb vigorous cultivar with small mid- to dark green foliage. It has small white self-coloured single flowers. It is that rare fuchsia: a white variety that stays white even in the full sun, with the flowers sparkling against the foliage. It is best placed at the back of the border because of its strong upright growth. In milder areas it will make a very large plant. Its parentage was *F. magellanica* var. *molinae* crossed with 'Venus Victrix'. Hardy; Zones 6–7. Growth 1.2m (4ft). Travis, UK, 1973.

'Hawkshead'

'Howlett's Hardy'

'Herald'

This is a strong upright-growing cultivar with attractive pale green foliage. It makes a very reliable garden plant for the middle of the hardy border and can also be used as a specimen plant in a large tub or container. The flowers are medium-sized singles with a medium-length bulbous red tube, recurved red sepals and a bluish-purple corolla with pink patches on the petals. The corolla fades to red as it ages. Hardy; Zones 6–7. Growth 60cm (2ft). Sankey, UK, 1895.

'Howlett's Hardy'

This upright and quite vigorous cultivar has medium-sized single flowers with a red tube and sepals, and a blue-violet corolla with paler pink patches at the base. The foliage is medium to large, mid-green and serrated. The flowers are of a good size for a hardy, and quite freely produced. It is a fuchsia to use in the centre of the hardy border, makes a nice pot plant and is very easy to grow to a half standard. It received an RHS Award of Garden Merit in 2005. Hardy; Zone 7. Growth 55cm (22in). Howlett, UK, 1952.

'Isabel Ryan'

This has strong upright bushy growth with medium-sized single flowers with a red tube, red recurving sepals and a white corolla with heavy red veining. The flowers stand out nicely against the dark green foliage. This attractive cultivar, raised in the Scilly Isles, was awarded a highly commended certificate in the 1975–78 RHS hardy trials, and has been assessed in the Netherlands as a good winter-hardy plant. Hardy; Zone 7. Growth 70cm (28in). Tabraham, UK, 1974.

'Isis'

One of three different cultivars named 'Isis', this entry refers to the one raised by de Groot, one of a series hybridized from *F. regia typica*, this one from a cross with 'Alice Hoffman'. It has upright growth and medium-sized single flowers with a red tube and sepals, and a purple corolla fading to reddish-purple with age. The leaf is an attractive dark green with a red midrib, and this fuchsia works well placed toward the front of a hardy border. Hardy; Zone 7. Growth 50cm (21in). de Groot, Netherlands, 1973.

'Isis'

'Jack Wilson'

This smaller growing floriferous cultivar makes a slightly lax bush with mid-green foliage, and is excellent at the front of the hardy border. The medium-sized single flowers have a medium to long white tube, white sepals that are pale pink underneath and a violet-cerise corolla with blue shading. Hardy; Zone 7. Growth 40cm (16in). Wilson, UK, 1979.

'Janna Roddenhof'

This hardy fuchsia is a cross between *F. regia typica* and 'Mood Indigo', and has quite an unusual colour. It has mid-green leaves, and the medium-sized single flowers have a red tube and sepals, and a beetroot-red corolla. A strong upright cultivar, it is useful in the middle of the border, but is not very widely available. Hardy; Zone 7. Growth 70cm (28in). de Groot, Netherlands, 1993.

'Joan Cooper'

The unusual colour combination of this fuchsia resulted from extensive work on hardy fuchsias by Mr W.P. Wood. It is a compact grower with attractive light green foliage, and has small single flowers with a pale rose-opal tube, fully reflexed pale rose-opal sepals and a cherry-red corolla.

'John E. Caunt'

It is a valuable addition to the range of hardy fuchsias, and is excellent for the front of a border with its spreading growth. Hardy; Zone 7. Growth 53cm (21in). Wood, UK, 1954.

'John E. Caunt'

A relatively new hardy, this is a slightly spreading upright bush with medium-sized, mid- to dark green foliage. The medium-sized single flowers have a red tube and sepals, and a flared magenta corolla. The flowers are held out well on the stem tips, creating an attractive bush. It received an RHS Award of Garden Merit in 2005. Hardy; Zone 7. Growth 55cm (22in). Caunt, UK, 1994.

'Kerry Ann'

This cultivar is an upright self-branching bush with mid-green foliage. The single flowers are medium-sized with a neyron-rose tube, neyron-rose sepals that curve upwards and an aster-violet corolla that is paler at the base of the petals. Although it is not listed as hardy in the UK, it has a hardy rating in the Netherlands, parts of which are Zones 7–8, so it is well worth trying. Hardy; Zones 7–8. Growth 60cm (2ft). Pacey, UK, 1971.

'Komeet'

This cultivar resulted from a cross between *F. regia typica* and 'Beacon', giving an upright plant with mid- to dark green foliage. The medium-sized single flowers have a short red tube, long narrow red sepals that droop down and a purple corolla maturing to lilac-red as the flower ages. It is a good strong growing plant that is suitable for the centre of the hardy border. Hardy; Zone 7. Growth 70cm (28in). de Groot, Netherlands, 1970.

'Joan Cooper'

'Komeet'

'Lady Thumb'

F. magellanica var. *gracilis*

'Lady Thumb'

This cultivar is a sport from 'Tom Thumb', inheriting many of its parent's characteristics but with very different flowers – small to medium semi-doubles, sometimes doubles, with reddish-light carmine tube and sepals and a fluffy white corolla. The foliage is mid-green and small in size and the growth bushy and compact. It is excellent for use in the rockery or as an edging plant, and can be grown to a superb miniature or quarter standard. Hardy; Zone 7. Growth 40cm (16in). Roe, UK, 1966.

'Liebriez'

This is a very old German cultivar. It has compact, somewhat lax upright growth forming a small dome with mid-green foliage. The plentiful small to medium-sized semi-double flowers have a pale red tube, reflexed pale red sepals and a pale pink corolla with red veining. It is good at the front of the border, as an edging plant and in the rockery. Hardy; Zone 7. Growth 26cm (10in). Kohne, Germany, 1874.

'Madame Cornelissen'

This strong upright shrub has small semi-double flowers with a red tube and sepals, and a milky-white corolla with red veining on the petals. It is very free-flowering with the small, dark green serrated foliage providing a nice contrast to the flowers. It is also very suitable for growing as a low dividing hedge in the garden. It received an RHS Award of Garden Merit in 1993. Hardy; Zones 7–8. Growth 60cm (2ft). Cornelissen, Belgium, 1860.

F. magellanica var. *gracilis*

This is one of the natural species variants of *F. magellanica*, also known in the USA as 'Senorita'. It has a vigorous, almost rampant, arching, slender growth with small, mid- to dark green leaves and single flowers that are slightly longer than

F. magellanica var. *pumila*

those of *F. magellanica* itself. The flowers are small with a red tube and sepals, and a deep purple corolla. This plant makes a very attractive specimen hardy shrub because of its arching growth, and is also suitable for growing as a hedge. This cultivar has an RHS Award of Garden Merit, awarded in 1993. Hardy; Zone 6. Growth 1m (3ft). Lindley, South America, 1824.

F. magellanica var. *molinae*

This is another of the natural species variants of *F. magellanica*, often sold as *F. magellanica alba*. In the USA it is known as 'Maiden's Blush'. Extremely hardy, this upright, strong and vigorous shrub with small light to mid-green bright foliage has small flowers with a white tube and sepals and a pale lilac corolla (nearer white in the shade). Hardy; Zone 6. Growth 1.2m (4ft). Espinosa, location not known, 1929.

F. magellanica var. *pumila*

This natural variant of *F. magellanica* is the smallest of the group. It has very small flowers with a scarlet tube and sepals and a purple corolla, and it grows into a small mound with small dark leaves, covered with tiny flowers. This fuchsia is best used at the front of the border or in a rockery. Hardy; Zone 6. Growth 45cm (18in). Country of origin and date unknown.

F. magellanica var. *riccartonii*

F. magellanica var. *riccartonii* ('Riccartonii')

There is some disagreement in the published literature about this fuchsia, and nurseries grow different fuchsias under this name. Often described as a *F. magellanica* variant, it was raised by James Young at the Riccarton estate in Scotland from a seed from 'Globosa' crossed with an unknown fuchsia, so more correctly it should be a cultivar. It is extremely hardy and vigorous, with small to medium single flowers with a red tube and narrow sepals held almost horizontally, and a dark purple corolla. This photograph is from the RHS garden at Wisley, England. Hardy; Zone 6. Growth 1.2m (4ft). Young, UK, 1830.

'Monsieur Thibaut'

This old French cultivar has medium-sized single flowers with a bulbous waxy red tube, broad waxy red sepals held horizontally and a mauve-purple corolla with paler patches at the base of the petals, which hardly fade. The growth is strong, vigorous and upright with dark green leaves, and it flowers early, profusely and fairly continuously. It will also make a

'Monsieur Thibaut'

nice standard that will grow quickly to the desired height because of its strong and vigorous habit. Hardy; Zones 6–7. Growth 85cm (33in). Lemoine, France, 1898.

'Mr A. Huggett'

This is a compact bushy cultivar that is very floriferous, usually covered in small, pretty single flowers. They have a short red tube, horizontal red sepals and a mauve corolla with a pronounced purple edge, being paler pink at the base of the petals. It is a good plant for the middle to front of the hardy border, and has upright, self-branching growth and mid-green foliage. It also works well as a pot plant or small standard. Hardy; Zone 7. Growth 68cm (27in). Raiser unknown, UK, 1930.

'Mrs Popple'

This excellent old hardy cultivar is one of the first fuchsias to flower each year, and one of the last to stop. It has vigorous upright growth with dark green serrated foliage and medium-sized single flowers with a short, thin scarlet tube, scarlet sepals and a violet-purple corolla with cerise veining. It is one of the most popular fuchsias, ideal for the hardy border, and

an exceptional cultivar for a fuchsia hedge. It received an RHS Award of Garden Merit in 1993. Hardy; Zone 6. Growth 1.2m (4ft). Elliot, UK, 1899.

'Nicola Jane'

This free-flowering bush cultivar has attractive medium-sized double flowers with a deep pink tube and sepals and a mauve-pink corolla, veined with cerise. The growth is upright and bushy, with mid-green foliage. It is a prettily coloured double-flowered cultivar that is very useful for growing toward the front of the hardy bed, and also makes an excellent shape when grown as a shrub in a pot. It is a useful addition to the range of hardy doubles. Hardy; Zone 7. Growth 40cm (16in). Dawson, UK, 1959.

'Nunthorpe Gem'

This newer hardy cultivar has an upright bushy shape with mid- to dark green foliage. The flowers are medium-sized doubles with a red tube, red sepals held horizontally and a deep purple corolla with red patches at the petal base. This hardy double is excellent for the centre of the hardy bed or used as summer bedding. Hardy; Zones 7–8. Growth 75cm (30in). Birch, UK, 1970.

'Mrs Popple'

'Papoose'

This is one of the few hardy fuchsias hybridized in the USA. It has a spreading habit, growing twice as wide as it is high, producing small but profuse semi-double flowers with a red tube and sepals, and a dark purple corolla. The small serrated leaves are mid-green. It is an excellent plant to grow in a rockery, and also suitable for a hanging pot. Hardy; Zone 7. Growth 40cm (16in). Reedstrom, USA, 1963.

'Pee Wee Rose'

This vigorous US cultivar grows with a rather lax, willowy habit. The flowers are small singles, sometimes semi-doubles, with a medium-length rose-red tube, short rose-red sepals drooping downwards and a rosy-mauve corolla. The rather small foliage is mid-green. Use in the centre of the hardy bed. This fuchsia is also very suitable to train as an espalier. Hardy; Zone 7. Growth 70cm (28in). Niederholzer, USA, 1939.

'Peggy King'

This hardy cultivar is a bushy self-branching upright with mid- to dark green foliage. The small single flowers are freely produced with a rose-red tube, rose-red sepals held slightly above the horizontal and a reddish-purple corolla, which fades

'Prosperity'

as the flower ages. A reliable fuchsia to position between the middle and back of the hardy border. Hardy; Zone 7. Growth 81cm (32in). Wood, UK, 1954.

'Prosperity'

This is a newer, vigorous, free-flowering hardy cultivar with medium-sized double flowers with a crimson tube and sepals, and a pale neyron-rose corolla with red veining on the petals. It has strong upright growth with medium to large dark green leaves. It will make a striking impression in the hardy bed, its double flowers being larger than those of most hardy fuchsias. It received an RHS Award of Garden Merit in 1993. Hardy; Zone 7. Growth 70cm (28in). Gadsby, UK, 1974.

'Reading Show'

This floriferous hardy cultivar has lovely medium-sized double flowers with a short red tube, long thick red sepals and a deep blue corolla, which is almost purple. It is an upright grower with mid- to dark green foliage very suitable for the front part of the hardy border. Hardy; Zones 7–8. Growth 45cm (18in). Wilson, UK, 1967.

'Red Ace'

This strong upright cultivar has yellowish-green foliage with distinct veining. With its vigorous growth, it makes an excellent specimen plant or one for the centre of a hardy border. The flowers are medium doubles and almost self-coloured with a dusky-red tube, dusky-red recurving sepals and a slightly darker dusky-red corolla that is very open. Its parentage is 'Rufus' x 'Herald', and it seems to have inherited the hardy characteristics of both parents. Hardy; Zone 7. Growth 65cm (26in). Roe, UK, 1983.

'Peggy King'

'Reading Show'

'Rufus'

'Rose of Castile'

One of the oldest hardy cultivars, this is still widely grown and well worth trying. The flowers are medium-sized singles with a white tube tinged with green, white sepals with green tips and a reddish-purple corolla with white patches at the base of the petals. The growth is vigorous, upright and bushy with mid-green foliage, and it is perfect for the middle of the hardy border. It can also be trained as a quarter or half standard. Hardy; Zone 7. Growth 46cm (18in). Banks, UK, 1855.

'Rufus'

This is a strong-growing hardy cultivar which develops naturally into an upright bush and is an early flowerer. The flower is a medium-sized single, almost a red self, with a red tube and turkey-red sepals and corolla. The foliage is mid-green with quite large leaves that are slightly serrated. It is suitable for the middle of the hardy border, or for training as a half standard. This cultivar is sometimes incorrectly named as 'Rufus the Red'. It is an easy one for the beginner to grow, and highly recommended. Hardy; Zones 6–7. Growth 50cm (21in). Nelson, USA, 1952.

'Saturnus'

This is a very hardy, good strong upright resulting from hybridization with *F. regia typica*, which forms a mound of dull green foliage covered in flowers. The latter are small singles with a red tube, long red sepals and a light purple corolla fading to mauve on maturity and veined with red. It received an Award of Garden Merit from the RHS in 2005 and the Dutch 'Ned-H3 goed winterhard' classification. Hardy; Zones 6–7. Growth 60cm (2ft). de Groot, Netherlands, 1970.

'Sealand Prince'

This hardy fuchsia is a strong grower that naturally forms an upright bushy shrub. It has medium-sized single flowers with a pink tube, long pink sepals and a violet-blue corolla with paler patches at the base of the petals. The medium-sized foliage is light green and contrasts nicely with the well-shaped flowers. This is a good plant for use between the middle and back of the hardy border. Hardy; Zones 6–7. Growth 75cm (30in). Walker, UK, 1967.

'Sleepy'

This low-growing plant is one of the Seven Dwarfs series raised by Tabraham in the Scilly Isles. Although listed as hardy, there is a debate over just how hardy it is. The flowers are small singles with a pale pink tube and sepals and a lavender-blue corolla. The growth is compact and low with small pale green leaves, so it works best at the front of the hardy border, in the rockery or as an edging plant. Hardy; Zone 8. Growth 26cm (10in). Tabraham, UK, 1954.

'Sealand Prince'

'Son of Thumb'

This cultivar is a dwarf-growing compact plant, one of the sports from the cultivar 'Tom Thumb'. It is ideal for growing at the front of the hardy border or in the rockery. The flowers are small singles with a cerise tube and sepals, and a lilac corolla. The foliage is small and mid-green, and the growth is bushy, self-branching and compact. As with the other cultivars in the Thumbs series, it is an excellent plant for growing a pretty miniature or quarter standard and as a pot plant. This cultivar has an RHS Award of Garden Merit, awarded in 1993. Hardy; Zone 7. Growth 30cm (12in). Gubler, UK, 1978.

'Son of Thumb'

'Tausendschön'

This is a rather small, self-branching upright bush with small to medium well-shaped double flowers with a shiny red tube and sepals that almost look as if they have been lacquered, and a light rose corolla veined red. The growth is compact with small mid- to dark green foliage. It is an ideal fuchsia for growing toward the front of the hardy border and the rockery, or as a miniature or quarter standard. It will also make a very pretty double-flowered compact pot plant. Hardy; Zone 7. Growth 40cm (16in). Nagel, Germany, 1919.

'Tennessee Waltz'

This is a very attractive hardy fuchsia. Although some references express doubts about its hardiness, testing in the Netherlands in an exposed Zone 7 site labelled it 'Ned-H3 goed winterhard' (truly winter hardy). Another factor, such as waterlogging could have affected its hardiness in other trials. The flower is a medium to large semi-double, but often has enough petals to be a double, with a red tube, rose-madder sepals and a lilac-lavender corolla splashed with rose. The

'Tennessee Waltz'

'The Tarns'

growth is upright, self-branching and bushy, with medium-sized light to mid-green leaves. It is an easy one for beginners to grow and will make a nice bush or larger standard. Hardy; Zones 7–8. Growth 60cm (2ft). Walker and Jones, USA, 1950.

'The Tarns'

This hardy cultivar has medium-sized single flowers with a short pink tube, long pink sepals and a violet-blue corolla with paler rose patches at the base of the petals. The growth is upright and bushy with medium-sized dark green foliage. Hardy; Zones 7–8. Growth 55cm (22in). Travis, UK, 1962.

'Thornley's Hardy'

This fuchsia is, unusually for a hardy cultivar, a trailing plant. This makes it difficult to use in the hardy border, but it can be grown instead on the edge of walls or similar places where it can trail downwards, and can also be used in baskets or hanging pots. The flowers are small singles with a waxy white tube, waxy white sepals and a red corolla. The growth is lax, with small mid-green leaves. It is

very floriferous and early-flowering. Hardy; Zones 7–8. Growth 30cm (12in). Thornley, UK, 1970.

'Variegated Pixie'

This variegated sport from 'Pixie', though less vigorous than its parent, does have interesting yellow and green leaves. The flowers are the same as the parent, being small singles with a cerise tube and sepals, and a rosy-mauve corolla with carmine veins. It makes an attractive variegated plant for the front of the border. Hardy; Zones 7–8. Growth 30cm (12in). Russell, UK, 1960.

'Vielliebchen'

This old German cultivar, the result of a cross between 'Charming' and *F. magellanica* var. *macrostemma*, is a strong upright with small mid-green foliage. The flowers are small singles with a red tube, shining red sepals and a dark purple corolla fading to red-purple. Because its height tends to exceed its spread, it is better used toward the back of the hardy border where its flowers will be seen. Hardy; Zones 6–7. Growth 81cm (32in). Wolf, Germany, 1911.

'Thornley's Hardy'

'Voltaire'

This old French hardy cultivar is a bushy upright that is still grown for its vivid and well-shaped flowers shining among the mid-green foliage. The flowers are medium-sized singles with a thick scarlet tube, slightly reflexed broad scarlet sepals and a beautifully contrasting pale magenta corolla with red veins. This is an excellent vigorous growing plant for the middle of the hardy border or simply to use as a summer bedder. Hardy; Zones 7–8. Growth 65cm (26in). Lemoine, France, 1897.

'Wharfedale'

This relatively new cultivar is listed as hardy in the UK, and resulted from a cross between 'Border Queen' and 'Celia Smedley'. It has very vigorous growth and forms a large bushy shrub that is quickly covered by mid-green foliage and flowers. The latter are medium-sized singles with a white tube, white sepals blushed with pink and a magenta corolla. Use it at the back of the border or as a specimen plant, and it probably also makes an excellent standard. Hardy; Zones 7–8. Growth 1m (3ft). Hanson, UK, 1993.

'Voltaire'

'White Pixie'

'White Pixie'

This reliable hardy cultivar was a sport from 'Pixie', which, in turn, was itself a sport from 'Graf Witte'. The upright, bushy self-branching growth is covered with attractive yellowish-green foliage with red veins. The flowers stand out well and are small singles with a short red tube, red sepals held horizontally and a white corolla veined with pink. It works well in the centre of the hardy border or as a small standard. Hardy; Zone 7. Growth 60cm (2ft). Merrist Wood, UK, 1968.

'Whiteknights Blush'

This hardy cultivar emerged from the work of J.O. Wright at Reading University and was the result from a hybridization cross between *F. magellanica* var. *molinae* and *F. fulgens*. It has compact upright bushy growth with small dark green foliage with paler green veins. The plentiful small single flowers have a pale pink tube, pale pink sepals with green tips and a clear pink corolla. It is happy in full sun and is excellent for the hardy border and summer bedding. Hardy; Zone 7. Growth 55cm (22in). Wright, UK, 1980.

'Whiteknights Pearl'

This is another cultivar from the work of John Wright, also originating from *F. magellanica* var. *molinae*. The flowers are rather similar to its parent, but somewhat larger, being small to medium-sized singles with a white tube, pale pink sepals with green tips and a pink corolla. The growth is vigorous, upright and bushy, with small dark green leaves and light green stems, excellent for the back of the hardy border. This fuchsia is very suitable for training as pyramids and pillars. Hardy; Zones 7–8. Growth 1m (3ft). Wright, UK, 1980.

'Wicked Queen'

This upright hardy cultivar is bushy and floriferous with dark green foliage. It has medium to large double flowers, quite large for a hardy, which start as a pointed bud and open to a flower with a red tube, red recurving sepals and a deep blue corolla splashed with pink. It is a good choice for the centre of the hardy border, growing as a half standard or a pot plant. Marketing of this cultivar is often in a group along with the Seven Dwarfs series and 'Snow White'. Hardy; Zones 7–8. Growth 70cm (28in). Tabraham, UK, 1985.

'Wicked Queen'

Summer bedding

Many fuchsias can be used in summer as temporary residents in a border, standing out with their strong shapes and beautiful flowers. Desirable characteristics include strong bushy growth and distinctive flowers. The following cultivars are among the best.

'Alde'

This is a strong-growing cultivar which does very well as a temporary resident in the summer border. It has small single flowers with a pale orange tube, pale orange sepals and an apricot corolla with attractive pleated petals. The medium-sized foliage is mid- to dark green and the growth is upright and slightly lax. This cultivar also grows well and looks very good in a half basket. Half hardy; Zones 9–10. Goulding, UK, 1989.

'Anita'

This is a vigorous bush cultivar with small to medium single flowers with a clear white tube, clear white sepals and an orange-red corolla. The growth is upright and self-branching with medium-sized

'Anita'

mid-green foliage, and it is very floriferous. It is an excellent plant for summer bedding or patio containers, being happy in full sun. There is another cultivar with the same name by Niederholzer, but this is a red and purple double. Half hardy; Zones 9–10. Götz, Germany, 1989.

'Beryl Shaffery'

This is a strong upright-growing cultivar with a good self-branching habit and mid-green medium-sized foliage. The erect single flowers have a pale pink tube and sepals, and the corolla is saucer-shaped with pink petals with a magenta blush. The well-displayed flowers make it excellent for temporary bedding, and it also makes a nice small standard. Half hardy; Zones 9–10. Shaffery, UK, 1997.

'Border Queen'

This is a striking fuchsia that should be included in any enthusiast's collection. With its good upright bushy and self-branching growth, with small to medium-sized mid-green leaves and red stems, it is excellent as a summer bedding plant, but will also make a lovely pot plant and is suitable for training into most shapes. The flowers are medium-sized singles

'Border Queen'

'Canny Bob'

with a short, pale pink tube, narrow pale pink sepals tipped green and an amethyst-violet corolla with pink veins on the petals. Half hardy; Zones 9–10. Ryle and Atkinson, UK, 1974.

'C.J. Howlett'

Small and hardy, this fuchsia makes a fine summer bedding plant, with its compact self-branching growth. Very floriferous, it has small single flowers with a reddish-pink tube, reddish-pink sepals tipped green and a bluish-carmine corolla with pink patches at the petal base. It tends to be early-flowering and sometimes throws additional semi-double flowers. Hardy; Zone 7. Growth 50cm (20in). Howlett, UK, 1911.

'Canny Bob'

This stiff and vigorous upright has small semi-erect single flowers with a white tube, white sepals and a glowing pink corolla. It grows long upright stems with small to medium-sized mid-green leaves with heavy clusters of flowers at the growing tips. It makes an excellent summer bedding, container or pot plant. Half hardy; Zones 9–11. Hewitson, UK, 1997.

'Chang'

'Chang'

This US cultivar, hybridized from
F. cordifolia, has profuse small single
flowers with an orange-red tube, orange
sepals tipped green and a brilliant
orange corolla. The growth is quite upright
with small to medium-sized mid-green
foliage. It thrives in the sun and does well
when planted out for the summer, with
continuous production of the orange-red
flowers. It is not easy to overwinter this
cultivar, so it is worth taking autumn
cuttings, which can be kept in growth over
the winter in a greenhouse as a precaution
against losing it during the winter
dormancy. Half hardy; Zones 9–10.
Hazard and Hazard, USA, 1946.

'Cloth of Gold'

This old cultivar was a sport from
'Souvenir de Chaswick', and is grown
more for its foliage than its flowers. It
grows quite vigorously as an upright bush,
and has beautiful golden-yellow and green
new foliage, which turns to a lovely bronze
colour with red on the underside on
ageing. The flowers are small singles with
a red tube and sepals, and a purple corolla
that is quite late to appear and rather
insignificant. This fuchsia is ideal for
creating a backdrop for other plants. Half
hardy; Zones 9–10. Stafford, UK, 1863.

'Dark Eyes'

This US cultivar grows as a slightly lax
self-branching bush with small to medium-
sized dark green foliage, and makes an
excellent border plant in summer. The
flowers are medium-sized doubles with a
short red tube, red upswept sepals and
a tight violet-blue corolla with rolled petals.
Try combining it with white-flowering
fuchsias or border bedding plants for
a bright contrast. It also works well as a
weeping standard. Half hardy; Zones
9–10. Erickson, USA, 1958.

'Dawn Fantasia'

This plant is one of a number of fuchsias
originally derived from the cultivar 'Pink
Fantasia'. It is a free-flowering variegated
sport from 'Rose Fantasia', itself a sport
from 'Pink Fantasia'. It is self-branching,
bushy and upright with cream margined
light to mid-green leaves. The small, erect
single flowers have a pale rose tube and
sepals, and a white corolla flushed with
pink. It is excellent for summer bedding
and pot plants. Half hardy; Zones 9–10.
Thornton, UK, 1999.

'Emily Austen'

This self-branching upright, bushy cultivar
has an abundance of small single flowers.
Each has a pale pink tube and sepals, and
a pink-orange corolla. It is an excellent
choice for summer bedding and pot
plants. Half hardy; Zones 9–10. Bielby
and Oxtoby, UK, 1990.

'Dark Eyes'

'Eternal Flame'

This US cultivar flowers profusely,
normally well into autumn, and even into
winter with the heat in a greenhouse or
conservatory. The attractive flowers are
medium-sized semi-doubles with a
salmon-pink tube, dark salmon-pink
sepals tipped green and a rose corolla
streaked orange. The growth is strong,
bushy and upright with medium-sized
dark green leaves, which are a perfect
foil to the flowers. It does extremely well
as a summer bedder, and is also good in
containers or as a standard. Half hardy;
Zones 9–10. Paskesen, USA, 1941.

'Dawn Fantasia'

'First Kiss'

'Golden Eden Lady'

'First Kiss'

This compact, upright bushy Dutch cultivar has rather square-shaped buds, and makes a nice pot plant or summer bedder. The flowers are medium to large semi-doubles with a cream tube, pale neyron-rose sepals tipped green and a half-flared rose corolla with a long, pale yellow style. The foliage is rather small and dark green, making a nice backdrop for the pale-coloured flowers. Half hardy; Zones 9–10. de Graff, Netherlands, 1985.

'Galadriel'

This strong upright bushy fuchsia makes an excellent bedding plant with the many flowers concentrated at the ends of the branches. The small single flowers have an ivory-white tube, horizontal ivory-white sepals and a cup-shaped orange-red corolla. The foliage is medium-sized and mid- to dark green. It has been tested and accepted in the Netherlands as a hardy cultivar. Hardy; Zones 7–8. de Graff, Netherlands, 1982.

'Golden Eden Lady'

This is a golden-leaf sport from the cultivar 'Eden Lady', sister seedling to 'Border Queen', with bright yellow leaves with green patches, but retaining almost the same flower. The flowers are medium-sized singles with a rose tube and sepals and a hyacinth-blue corolla. It makes a very good summer bedding plant, especially where a change in foliage colour helps the planting scheme. Half hardy; Zones 9–10. Cater, UK, 1982.

'Golden Treasure'

This fuchsia has the habit of a low-growing bush, with very attractive green and gold foliage highlighted with red veins. Both the

'Galadriel'

growth and the colour make it ideal for edging. The small single flowers are rather sparse, with a scarlet tube and sepals, and a purple corolla. Hardy; Zone 7. Carter, UK, 1860.

'Gwen Dodge'

This fuchsia has stiff upright growth and pretty single flowers, making it ideal for summer bedding. The semi-erect medium-sized flowers have a white tube and sepals, both of which flush with pink in the sun, and a lilac-blue to purple flared corolla that is white at the petal base. The medium-sized foliage is mid-green, and this cultivar is very floriferous. Half hardy; Zones 9–10. Dyos, UK, 1988.

'Hiawatha'

This Dutch cultivar has compact, upright and bushy free-flowering growth, and makes an excellent small pot plant or summer bedder. The small single flowers have a short white tube and sepals, both flushed with rose, and a dark red corolla. The foliage is small and mid-green, and it happily takes the full sun and starts flowering very early in the season. This cultivar was a seedling from 'La Campanella' parentage. Half hardy; Zones 9–10. van Wijk, Netherlands, 1984.

'Ian Brazewell'

'Honnepon'

This semi-lax upright thrives in sunny areas, producing an abundance of flowers. The small single blooms are held outwards with a white corolla tinged pink, white sepals shaded with mauve and tipped green, and a purple-mauve corolla with pink patches at the petal base. The medium-sized foliage is olive green and has red stems. Half hardy; Zones 9–10. Brouwer, Netherlands, 1988.

'Ian Brazewell'

This is a very vigorous upright, bushy fuchsia that flowers very early and makes a good summer bedder, pot plant or standard. The flowers are medium-sized doubles with a claret-rose tube and sepals, and a plum-purple corolla. The stamens hang down well below the corolla. The medium-sized foliage is mid-green and an excellent foil for the abundant flowers. Half hardy; Zones 9–10. Day, UK, 1988.

'Ingram Maid'

This is an almost white-flowered cultivar which tolerates the sun very well, maintaining its colours. It has strong upright growth with medium-sized mid-green leaves, and benefits from some early pinching. The medium-sized single flower has a white tube, white sepals flushed with rose and held outwards, and a creamy white corolla. Half hardy; Zones 9–10. Ryle, UK, 1976.

'Jack King'

A sport from the old French hardy cultivar 'General Monk', this is more vigorous and with slightly larger flowers. It tolerates the sun very well and therefore makes an excellent bedding plant. Although not recognized as a hardy, it might be worth trying in milder areas because sports tend to inherit many characteristics of the parent. The flowers are medium-sized doubles with a crimson tube and sepals, and a flared lilac corolla, the petals having rose veins with pink at the base. Growth is upright with medium-sized mid-green leaves. Half hardy; Zones 9–10. Holmes, UK, 1978.

'Jack Siverns'

This is a superb cultivar from a hybridizer normally famed for his compact small-flowered introductions. It is a very strong upright, being self-branching and extremely floriferous, and makes a terrific pot plant or standard, also being ideal for bedding outdoors in the summer. The medium-sized, classically shaped single flowers have a pink tube, pale pink upswept sepals flushed with aubergine and a beautiful, tight bell-shaped aubergine corolla. The small to medium-sized foliage is mid- to dark green. This cultivar is likely to become very popular as its fame spreads. Half hardy; Zones 9–10. Reynolds, UK, 2001.

'Jack Siverns'

'John Bartlett'

This newish cultivar is very floriferous and frequently throws three flowers in succession from each leaf joint. The plant is also quite self-cleaning of seedpods, which means that the residual ovaries from the old flowers fall off before growing into berries. The flowers are medium-sized semi-erect singles with a red tube and sepals, and a white corolla with red veining on the petals. The foliage is medium-sized and dark green. It is worth growing this cultivar as a standard, or as a temporary summer resident in the border where it will flower all summer. Half hardy; Zones 9–10. Humphries, UK, 2003.

'John Bartlett'

'Ken Jennings'

Upright, bushy and strong, this fuchsia makes a good pot or bedding plant in summer. The medium-sized single flowers have a pink tube, rhodamine-pink sepals held horizontally and a deep purple corolla. The medium-sized leaves are mid-green. Half hardy; Zones 9–10. Roe, UK, 1982.

'Kleine Gärtnerin'

This is an upright self-branching cultivar with mid- to dark green foliage, which is quite happy in full sun. It has medium-sized semi-double to double flowers with a white tube striped green, white sepals tinged with pink at the base and a white corolla tinged with pink at the base. It is suitable for summer bedding or as a pot plant. Half hardy; Zones 9–10. Strümper, Germany, 1985.

'Leo Goetelen'

This strong-growing upright fuchsia with some similarities to 'Celia Smedley' thrives in full sun. It has medium to large single flowers with a cream tube tinged pink, pink sepals tipped green and a smoky-red corolla. The flowers stand out well against the medium-sized light to mid-green leaves with their serrated edges. It is very good as a summer bedding plant and grows well as a standard. Half hardy; Zones 9–10. Tamerus, Netherlands, 1987.

'Lydia Götz'

'Lydia Götz'

This German cultivar is popular as a summer bedder in many parts of Europe. It is upright and bushy with medium-sized mid- to dark green foliage. The flowers are medium-sized singles with a red tube, red sepals held out horizontally and a very pretty lilac-blue corolla. Half hardy; Zones 8–9. Götz, Germany, 1958.

'Margaret Hazelwood'

With its compact, upright and self-branching growth, this fuchsia is an attractive summer bedder. The small flowers are erect singles with a deep pink tube, deep pink sepals and a very pale lilac-purple corolla. The small foliage is an attractive light to mid-green shade, and it is excellent as a small pot plant or trained as a small standard. Half hardy; Zones 8–9. Storey, UK, 1997.

'Minirose'

This plant is small and compact but also quite vigorous. It is early-flowering, and continues to flower well over a long period. The flowers are small singles that are held outwards and have a white tube blushed with rose, white sepals blushed with rose and a dark cyclamen-purple corolla. The foliage is small to medium in size and light to mid-green in colour. It grows well in pots, makes effective smaller standards and is quite happy in the border over the summer. Half hardy; Zones 9–10. de Graaff, Netherlands, 1985.

'Ken Jennings'

'Minirose'

'Nice 'n' Easy'

'Nicis Findling'

'Mrs W. Castle'

This is a strong and upright cultivar which is very floriferous and tolerates full sun. The flowers are medium singles, sometimes semi-doubles, with a red tube and sepals, and a pinkish-mauve corolla. The flowers contrast well with the dark green foliage, making this a good summer bedder and pot plant. Some catalogues claim it is hardy. Hardy; Zone 8. Growth 60cm (24in). Porter, UK, 1984.

'Nice 'n' Easy'

This is an upright, self-branching, compact fuchsia that is very floriferous and, as its name suggests, easy to grow. The flowers are medium-sized doubles with a carmine tube, carmine sepals held out horizontally and a white corolla veined carmine. The foliage is medium-sized, mid-green and quite narrow. It is excellent as a bedding plant in summer, and also makes a good standard or pot plant. Half hardy; Zones 9–10. Sinton, UK, 1988.

'Nicis Findling'

The spelling of this cultivar's name varies in many catalogues and references. It is frequently listed as 'Nicki's Findling', 'Nickis Findling' or 'Nici's Findling', but according to German references the spelling above is correct. It is an excellent summer bedding cultivar with strong upright growth, tolerating hot, dry conditions well. The small single flowers are held semi-erect and are produced towards the ends of the branches. They have an orange-rose tube and sepals, and a deeper orange corolla. The flowers contrast nicely with the medium to large mid-green foliage. Half hardy; Zones 9–10. Ermel, Germany, 1985.

'Other Fellow'

This cultivar flowers extremely well and makes an excellent plant for the border over the summer, with its long, continuous flowering period. The flowers are small singles with a long waxy white tube, waxy white sepals tipped with green and a coral-pink corolla. The growth is upright and quite vigorous, with medium-sized mid-green serrated leaves. This fuchsia is also worth growing as a pot plant, a quarter or half standard or in mixed containers. Half hardy; Zones 9–10. Hazard and Hazard, USA, 1946.

'Peter Bielby'

A very vigorous upright fuchsia, this needs plenty of pinching out at an early stage, and will then make a good bush relatively quickly. It also makes an excellent bedding plant with its medium to large double flowers with a long thin red tube, long recurving red sepals and a full purple-red corolla with salmon splashes on the petals. The flowers contrast against the quite large light to mid-green foliage. Half hardy; Zones 9–10. Bielby, UK, 1987.

'Pink Fantasia'

This cultivar made a tremendous impact on its first release, and it is now quite widely grown both as an exhibition plant and for garden displays. The medium-sized erect single flowers have a pinkish-red tube and sepals, and a violet to mauve corolla. The growth is upright and bushy with medium-sized mid- to dark green foliage, and it produces many flowers over a long period. Because of its erect-flowering habit, it makes an excellent plant for the summer border, but it will also make a striking standard or pot plant, which at its peak of flowering almost makes the leaves invisible. Half hardy; Zones 9–10. Webb, UK, 1989.

'Pink Fantasia'

'Queen's Park'

This is quite a free-flowering older cultivar with an upright bushy habit and mid-green foliage. It is happy in full sun and therefore excellent for summer bedding. The medium to large double flowers have a waxy red tube and sepals, and a full violet corolla. It is not that easy to find, but is still listed in some larger nursery catalogues and well worth searching for. Half hardy; Zones 9–10. Thorne, UK, 1959.

'Ravensbarrow'

This cultivar flowers very early in the year, and stays in flower for the whole summer. Although the single flowers are small they have a very good form, with a short scarlet tube, slightly reflexed scarlet sepals and a purple corolla with scarlet patches at the base of the petals. It is an upright-growing shrub with small mid- to dark green leaves and although not listed as a hardy, one of its parents is 'Hawkshead' so it may be worth trying as a hardy plant in milder areas. Note that in some catalogues it is erroneously referred to as 'Raven's Barrow'. Half hardy; Zones 9–10. Thornley, UK, 1972.

'Rose Fantasia'

This cultivar is a sport of 'Pink Fantasia', and perhaps actually more suited to its parent's name. It has almost the same

'Shanley'

growth habit as its parent, but the flower is a much softer colour. It has a medium erect single flower with a deep pink tube and sepals, and a pale pink corolla with a hint of mauve. The foliage is still a mid-green, a shade or two lighter than 'Pink Fantasia', and it is still very free-flowering. Like its parent, it is excellent for use in summer bedding schemes, as a pot plant or trained as a standard. Half hardy; Zones 9–10. Wilkinson, UK, 1991.

'Shanley'

This cultivar has attractive medium to large single flowers with a long, pale salmon-orange tube, pale salmon-orange sepals

with green tips, held horizontally, and an orange corolla. With its strong upright growth it makes a good bedding plant, with the flowers standing out against the large ovate mid-green leaves. It is happy growing in a sunny position. Half hardy; Zones 9–10. Mrs Shutt (Jnr), USA, 1968.

'Sharon Allsop'

This is a very floriferous compact cultivar that is ideal as a smaller pot plant and garden bedder, when combined with low-growing plants. The flowers are medium-sized doubles with a short carmine tube and downward-curving carmine sepals that cup the fluffy white corolla. The flowers stand out well against the small mid- to dark green leaves, making a neat mound of colour. Half hardy; Zones 9–10. Pacey, UK, 1983.

'Superstar'

This is a superb upright, bushy short-jointed cultivar with attractive light green foliage. It is very floriferous, with small to medium-sized semi-erect single flowers with a pink tube, pink sepals tipped green and an attractive rose-purple corolla. It is an excellent cultivar, suitable for pot plants and small standards, and the sun tolerance inherited from one of its parents, 'Cambridge Louie', makes it a good bedding plant for summer use. Half hardy; Zones 9–10. Sinton, UK, 1988.

'Rose Fantasia'

'Superstar'

'WALZ Jubelteen'

'Welsh Dragon'

'Ted Sweetman'
This cultivar from New Zealand, named after a well-known fuchsia personality there, will make a very nice pot plant or a bedding plant for the border in the summer. The flower is a medium-sized double with a cream tube, cream sepals flushed green and pink, and a violet corolla flushed pink. The growth is upright and bushy, and the foliage is medium to large and a shade of greyish-green. Half hardy; Zones 9–10. Sharpe and Proffitt, New Zealand, 1988.

'WALZ Jubelteen'
This is an erect-flowering fuchsia, a strong upright bushy grower that is quite happy in full sun and is extremely floriferous. The small single flowers have a pale pink tube, pale pink sepals with green tips and a pinkish-orange corolla that is flared almost flat when fully open. The foliage is medium-sized light to mid-green. It is excellent as a specimen pot plant, most standard sizes except miniature, and in summer bedding schemes. Half hardy; Zones 9–10. Waldenmaier, Netherlands, 1990.

'Waveney Waltz'
This bushy upright and self-branching cultivar with light green foliage makes a good pot plant and an attractive summer bedding plant. The flowers are medium-sized singles with a short pink tube, pink sepals held out horizontally and a white corolla. It will occasionally produce extra petals, giving semi-double flowers. It is also well worth trying growing it as a standard, especially a quarter standard. Half hardy; Zones 9–10. Burns, UK, 1982.

'Welsh Dragon'
With its strong upright bushy growth, this fuchsia tolerates full sun, so is excellent for summer bedding. The flowers are large doubles with a long rose-red tube, rose-red sepals held horizontally and a full magenta-rose corolla with the petals in layers. It is very free-flowering for a large double, and the medium-sized mid-green leaves contrast well with the flowers. It is good for pot plants and larger standards. This is one of those cultivars where the flowers drag the branches down, so it can be used in the centre of baskets. Half hardy; Zones 9–10. Baker, UK, 1970.

'White Ann'
This cultivar is a sport from 'Heidi Ann' – it shows the same growth characteristics but with different flower colours. Note that an almost identical sport named 'Heidi Weiss' is separately registered. The growth is upright and bushy, with mid- to dark green foliage, and the flowers are medium-sized doubles with a crimson tube and sepals, and a white, crimson-veined corolla. It is well worth growing in the border or in pots. Half hardy; Zones 8–9. Wills and Atkinson, UK, 1972.

'Zets Alpha'
This is an unusual cultivar for use as a bedding plant. It resulted from a hybridization cross between *F. vulcanica* and 'Citation', and has an upright vigorous habit with medium to large light to mid-green leaves, and produces a mass of flowers. The latter are medium-sized singles with a very long red tube, short rose-red sepals and an orange-red corolla. This fuchsia is very tolerant of a sunny position, making it highly suitable for summer bedding. Half hardy; Zones 9–10. Stoel, Netherlands, 1993.

'White Ann'

Species fuchsias

The species fuchsias grow in the wild in South and Central America, Mexico and New Zealand, and will grow true from seed. Many are tender, but some are quite hardy, and there is a tremendous variety of colour and form. Species are still being discovered in South America.

F. arborescens
This is found in Mexico and southern Peru at altitudes of 1,700–2,500m (5,570–8,200ft), where it grows as a large shrub or small tree up to 8m (26ft) tall. The tiny single flowers are held upright in panicles and have a rose-purple tube and sepals, and a lavender corolla eventually maturing to clusters of purple globular berries. The large glossy foliage is mid- to dark green. Often known as the lilac fuchsia, it is easy to grow but must not be allowed to dry out. Section Schufia; Tender; Zone 11. Sims, Mexico, 1825.

F. andrei
Found from southern Ecuador to northern Peru at altitudes of 1,800–3,000m (5,900–9,800ft), this is a shrub up to 4m (13ft) tall. The medium-sized single flowers are held in terminal racemes with a medium-length orange to red tube, horizontal red sepals and an orange-red

F. andrei

F. arborescens

corolla. The leaves are mid-green with a waxy texture, and are normally arranged in opposite pairs. Section Fuchsia; Tender; Zone 11. Johnston, Ecuador, 1925.

F. boliviana var. boliviana
The habitat of this fuchsia is spread from northern Argentina to southern Peru at altitudes of 1,000–3,000m (3,300–9,800ft), where it grows as a large shrub or small tree up to 4.5m (15ft) tall. The single flowers are held in large pendulous groups at the growing tips, with a 7.5cm (3in) long red tube, short reflexed red sepals and a red corolla. The large mid-green leaves have a hairy texture and red veining. Section Fuchsia; Frost tender; Zone 11. Carrière, Brazil, 1876.

F. coccinea
Naturally occurring in Brazil at altitudes of 1,400–2,000m (4,600–6,600ft), this grows as a dense shrub up to 1.5m (5ft) tall. The small single flowers have a pale red tube and sepals, and a violet corolla. The oval foliage is dark green on the top side, paler green beneath and the young branches are thin, red and covered with fine hair. Section Quelusia; Hardy; Zones 6–7. Drylander, Brazil, 1789.

F. denticulata

F. decussata
This fuchsia is found in Peru at altitudes of 2,900–3,400m (9,600–11,200ft), where it grows up to 3m (10ft) tall as a shrub with a lot of self-branching. The flowers are small to medium-sized singles with a dark red tube and sepals, and an orange-red corolla produced somewhat sparsely in the leaf axils, with small dark green foliage. Section Fuchsia; Frost tender; Zone 11. Ruiz and Pavon, Peru, 1802.

F. denticulata
This fuchsia comes from Peru and Bolivia at altitudes of 2,800–3,500m (8,200–11,500ft), where it grows up to 4m (13ft) tall. The dark green spear-shaped leaves usually grow in groups of three, with very attractive medium-sized single flowers appearing in the leaf axils. The flowers have a long, light pink-red tube with green at the tips and an orange to scarlet corolla. Most of the flowers appear in spring and autumn, sparser in the summer. This is an easy species for the beginner to try as a pot plant that is a little more frost-tolerant than many species. It was formerly known as *F. serratifolia*. Section Fuchsia; Half hardy; Zones 9–10. Ruiz and Pavon, Peru, 1802.

F. encliandra subsp. encliandra

This is found from Mexico to Panama at altitudes of 1,370–3,200m (4,500–10,500ft), where it grows up to 2.5m (8ft) tall. The profuse tiny single flowers are normally red with both staminate (male) and pistillate (female) flowers. The fern-like foliage is small and mid- to dark green. Section Encliandra; Hardy; Zones 8–9. Steudel, Mexico, 1840.

F. excorticata

This is found in both islands of New Zealand growing at altitudes of 1,000m (3,300ft), where it is a deciduous tree up to 15m (50ft) tall. A common tree in New Zealand, it is easily recognized by its distinctive cinnamon-brown bark, which peels in long strips, and the glossy leaves which are medium to dark green on top and light green, or sometimes white, beneath. The small single flowers have a tube and sepals that turn from green to purple-red and a dark purple corolla with distinctive blue pollen on the anthers. Section Skinnera; Half hardy; Zone 9. Forster, New Zealand, 1781.

F. fulgens

This fuchsia from Mexico occurs in humid areas beside flowing water at elevations of 1,450–2,300m (4,450–7,550ft), growing as a shrub 0.6–6.1m (2–20ft) tall. It has tuberous roots, often growing epiphytically in damp crevices and trees, and sheds its large light green foliage in

F. excorticata

dry seasons. The long single flowers are held in terminal clusters with a long dark pink to dull red tube, short pale red sepals with yellow-green tips and a bright red corolla. Section Ellobium; Tender; Zone 11. De Candolle, Mexico, 1828.

F. glazioviana

This fuchsia is from the highlands of eastern Brazil at altitudes of 1,500–2,000m (4,900–6,600ft), where it grows up to 4m (13ft) high with long spreading branches. The mid-green ternate leaves are quite shiny and appear in opposite pairs or in threes. The ends of the branches carry the small to medium-sized single flowers, which have a deep pink tube, deep pink sepals and a violet corolla.

It is a useful hybridization parent because of its natural resistance to many of the pests and diseases that afflict modern cultivars. Section Quelusia; Half hardy; Zones 9–10. Taubert, Brazil, 1888.

F. hatschbachii

This is found in the forests of eastern Brazil at altitudes of 900–1,200m (3,000–3,900ft), where it grows up to 5m (16ft) high as a climbing shrub. The flowers are small to medium-sized singles with a red tube, drooping red sepals and a violet corolla. The foliage is light to mid-yellow-green. Section Quelusia; Tender; Zone 11. Berry, Brazil, 1989.

F. jimenezii

A fairly recent discovery and the only current member of the Jimenezia section, this fuchsia comes from Panama and Costa Rica on the fringes of evergreen cloud forests at altitudes of 1,500–1,900m (4,900–6,200ft), where it grows up to 1.5m (5ft) high as a climbing shrub. It is named after its discoverer, Alfonso Jiménez Muñoz, and was first described by Breedlove, Berry and Raven in 1976. It has tiny single flowers held mainly in terminal racemes, with a red tube and sepals and a pink corolla. The foliage is quite large and dark green, being flushed purple underneath. Section Jimenezia; Tender; Zone 11. Muñoz, Panama/Costa Rica, 1967.

F. fulgens

F. hatschbachii

F. magellanica

F. magellanica

From the central and southern Andes, this fuchsia grows between sea level and altitudes of 1,750m (5,700ft). This species, from which many modern cultivars originate, grows as an erect or semi-scandent shrub up to 3m (9ft) tall. The profuse small single flowers have a red tube and drooping sepals, and a purple corolla on wiry branches with small, thin, dark green leaves. Widely grown in cultivation and very hardy, it makes an excellent hedge. Section Quelusia; Hardy; Zone 6. Lamarck, Chile, 1768.

F. obconica

From the lower mountains of the trans-Mexican volcanic belt at altitudes of 1,675–2,450m (5,500–8,000ft), this fuchsia is a tall, spreading shrub that grows 1–3m (3–10ft) high. One of the more recently discovered species, it has tiny single flowers, both staminate (male) and pistillate (female), with a greenish-white tube and sepals, and a white corolla. It has small, ovate mid-green leaves that are slightly larger than typical Encliandras. The plant is easy to grow and readily available from specialist nurseries. Section Encliandra; Half hardy; Zones 9–10. Bredlove, Mexico, 1969.

F. paniculata subsp. *paniculata*

F. paniculata subsp. *paniculata*

From southern Mexico to Panama, this fuchsia varies from a shrub growing to 2.5m (8ft) to a tree growing to 7.5m (25ft) in evergreen cloud forests at altitudes of 1,220–3,000m (4,000–10,000ft). The tiny single flowers are both perfect (male and female parts) and pistillate (female), held in terminal racemes with a rose-purple tube and sepals, and a lavender corolla. The large deep green shiny leaves are serrated on the edges, while the flowering racemes form globular purple berries with a waxy-blue bloom. It needs a warm position to grow well, and tends to lose berries and flowers with large temperature variations. Section Schufia; Tender; Zone 11. Lindley, Costa Rica, 1856.

F. petiolaris

This is found in Colombia and Venezuela, where it grows at altitudes of 2,900–3,900m (9,500–12,800ft) varying from a low shrubby bush 0.6–2m (2–6ft) tall to a climbing tree up to 5m (16ft). The single flowers have a long bright pink tube, bright pink sepals tipped green and a bright rose-pink corolla. The ternate leaves are dull mid-green on top and lighter beneath, held on dark pink stems. It likes warm conditions and takes longer to establish than other species, but it will flower all summer. Section Fuchsia; Frost tender; Zone 11. Humbolt and Bonpland, Colombia, 1823.

F. procumbens

From the northern part of the north island of New Zealand, this fuchsia spreads and trails up to 6m (20ft) wide but grows just 23cm (9in) high. The tiny erect flowers have a greenish-yellow tube and green sepals tipped purple. There is no corolla but the upright stamens carry blue pollen. Many of the fertilized flowers grow to become very attractive large pink-red fruits. The small, light green heart-shaped leaves are borne on slender stalks attached to thin trailing stems growing a few metres (yards) long. It is quite hardy and a good ingredient in rockeries. Section Procumbentes; Hardy; Zone 7. Cunningham, New Zealand, 1834.

F. sessifolia

Found in Ecuador and Colombia at altitudes of 2,300–3,200m (7,500–10,500ft), this grows as a shrub or small tree to a height of 3m (10ft). The large dark green leaves are sessile (without stalks), hence the name, and the young branches are dark red. The single flowers are held in terminal clusters and have a long light red or pink tube, greenish-red sepals and a scarlet corolla. Section Fuchsia; Tender; Zone 11. Bentham, Ecuador, 1845.

F. petiolaris

F. simplicicaulis

From central Peru, this fuchsia grows in cloud forests at altitudes of 2,400m (8,000ft) where it is a vigorous climbing species, sending its scandent 5m (16ft) long growth through adjacent shrubs and trees. The single flowers, held in pendent racemes, have a long reddish-pink tube, short reddish-pink sepals and a bright red corolla. The leaves are darkish green with a satin texture, while the mature wood is light red with peeling bark. Section Fuchsia; Tender; Zone 11. Ruiz and Pavon, Peru, 1802.

F. splendens

This is from Mexico and Costa Rica at altitudes of 2,400–3,400m (7,900–11,100ft), where it grows in moist forests as a lax shrub up to 2.4m (8ft) tall and, occasionally, as an epiphytic plant on trees. The single flowers have a distinctive flat tube varying from rose to vivid scarlet, short green sepals with a reddish base and an olive-green corolla. The leaves are dull mid-green with marbled veining. It flowers all year in its natural habitat, but in northern Europe and the northern USA it tends to flower in the darker months. Section Ellobium; Frost tender; Zone 11. Zuccarini, Costa Rica, 1832.

F. thymifolia subsp. thymifolia

This fuchsia is found in Mexico at altitudes of 2,130–3,350m (7,000–11,000ft). It is a shrub with tiny single flowers with a greenish-white tube and sepals turning pink, and a white to pink corolla turning purple after fertilization. Section Encliandra; Hardy; Zone 7. Humbolt, Bonpland and Kunth, Mexico, 1823.

F. triphylla

This species exists in Haiti and grows as a shrub up to 2m (6ft) tall. It is one of the most difficult fuchsias to cultivate. It has Triphylla-type orange-red flowers held in terminal racemes with dull dark green foliage, and can flower when barely 30cm (12in) tall. It is a interesting one to try growing. Section Fuchsia; Tender; Zone 11. Plumier, Haiti, 1703.

F. splendens

F. venusta

Growing naturally in Colombia and Venezuela at altitudes of 1,800–2,700m (5,900–8,850ft), this is one of the most beautiful species fuchsias. It grows as an upright spreading shrub to 3m (10ft) tall or climbs through trees up to a height of 10m (33ft). The single flowers have a long orange-red trumpet-shaped tube, orange-red sepals tipped green and an orange corolla. Glossy elliptical dark green leaves, lighter beneath, appear ternately (in groups of three) on red to bluish stems, and the mature wood has attractive peeling bark. The flowers appear axially singly and terminally in sub-racemes (small groups).

F. thymifolia subsp. thymifolia

The plant enjoys even, warm conditions without large extremes in temperature, and does not like overwatering when it is young. Section Fuchsia; Tender; Zone 11. Humbolt, Bonpland and Kunth, Colombia, 1823.

F. vulcanica

Occurring in southern Columbia and Ecuador at altitudes of 3,340–4,000m (11,000–13,000ft), this fuchsia grows up to 4m (13ft) high. The long single flowers have a long thin orange tube, orange-red sepals tipped green and a red corolla. The foliage is dark matt green and the bark peels on older branches. Section Fuchsia; Tender; Zone 11. André, Ecuador, 1876.

F. triphylla

Unusual cultivars

If you are looking for something different, try growing some of these unusual cultivars. Many are produced by crossing fuchsia species and are quite tender, so in temperate climates they will need the protection of a heated greenhouse over the winter.

'Cotta Christmas Tree'
Produced by hybridizing two fuchsia species, *F. decussata* and *F. crassistipula*, this has upright spreading growth and almost naturally grows to a pyramid shape with flowers resembling hanging candles. The medium-sized single flowers are similar to those of *F. decussata* and have a long, tapered red tube, red sepals with green tips and an orange corolla. The foliage is medium-sized and mid- to dark green. Frost tender; Zone 11. Bielby and Oxtoby, UK, 1999.

'Daryn John Woods'
This Triphylla-type fuchsia has a most unusual flower colour and was produced by hybridizing 'Thalia' and *F. juntasensis*. The medium-sized Triphylla-type flowers are borne in terminal clusters and have a long aubergine-purple tube, short

'Fulpila'

'Lechlade Gorgon'

aubergine-purple sepals and a purple corolla. The foliage is quite large and dark green and, with its bushy growth habit, it makes a nice pot plant. Be patient, because it is rather late to flower. Frost tender; Zone 11. Goulding, UK, 2000.

'Delta's Drop'
This Dutch cultivar is an upright bushy grower that benefits from early pinching, with mid- to dark green foliage. The unusual eye-catching flowers are small to medium-sized singles with a red tube and sepals, and a purple corolla with a red base to the petals, which become petaloids growing as part of the outer anthers as the flower matures. Grow it in a shady position to get the best colours, because it can be bleached by too much sun. Half hardy; Zones 9–10. Vreeke and van't Westeinde, Netherlands, 1994.

'Fulpila'
This vigorous fuchsia, produced by hybridization between *F. fulgens* and *F. pilaloensis*, has spreading upright growth, and is ideal for a patio container. The long single flowers are held in terminal clusters with a long pale pink-orange tube, short pale pink-orange sepals tipped green and an orange corolla. The velvety foliage is light to mid-green. Tender; Zone 11. Beije, Netherlands, 1997.

'Lechlade Gorgon'
This large upright with 9–15cm (3½–5in) dark green glossy leaves makes a good patio pot plant. Hybridized by crossing *F. arborescens* with *F. paniculata*, it has the same type of paniculate flower clusters as its parents. The individual tiny single flowers have a rosy purple tube and sepals, and a pale mauve corolla with erect petals. With plenty of feeding and a large root run, it will put on a lot of growth in a season. Tender; Zones 10–11. Wright, UK, 1984.

'Martin's Yellow Surprise'
This unusual tender cultivar is an interspecies cross of *F. pilaloensis* x *F. fulgens* and forms a large-growing bush. The flowers are a good-sized Triphylla type – while not growing as true terminal clusters, they are concentrated at the ends of the branches. The tube and sepals are green-yellow, though they can take on a pink blush in full sun, and the corolla is green-yellow, though always partially hidden by the sepals. Its growth is upright and quite vigorous with large felt-like mid-green leaves. As the plant is quite tender, it needs a well-heated greenhouse over the winter. It is an unusual plant which can be grown as a specimen on the patio in the summer. Tender; Zone 11. Beije, Netherlands, 1995.

'Martin's Yellow Surprise'

'Nettala'

'Space Shuttle'

'Nettala'

This fuchsia was a sport from the cultivar 'Chang' and shares similar characteristics, being upright and strong-growing with mid-green foliage. It is distinguished by the flowers, which are small to medium-sized singles with a short dark red tube, dark red sepals and a violet-red corolla with the petals being petaloids growing as part of the outer anthers. Half hardy; Zones 9–10. Francesca, USA, 1973.

'Rose Quartet'

With its unusual flowers, this new cultivar created quite a stir when it was released in the USA, and it is now available in other countries. The breeder assigned the rights to Planthaven Inc. in the USA, where it is subject to a patent. The flowers are small to medium-sized erect singles with a pink tube and sepals, and a rose corolla; the petals are petaloids growing as part of the outer anthers, which rapidly extend when the buds open. The growth is upright, self-branching and bushy, with a young plant growing 60cm (2ft) a season. In the patent it is claimed to survive outdoors in Zone 9 areas, but it should be treated as half hardy until more details are known. Half hardy; Zones 9–10. Spanton, UK, 2006.

'Space Shuttle'

This Dutch cultivar is the result of crossing 'Speciosa' and *F. splendens*, and has the growth habit of a lax bush. It starts to flower early and has a long flowering period, with small to medium-sized single flowers with a medium to long red tube, short downward-pointing red sepals tipped green and a yellow-red corolla. The quite large foliage is light to mid-green, with a slightly furry matt surface that is heavily veined. Half hardy; Zones 9–10. de Graaff, Netherlands, 1981.

'Tarra Valley'

This unusual cultivar is an interspecies cross between *F.* x *colensoi* and *F. splendens*, and one for the collector. The buds are yellow-green and the flowers small singles with a long light greenish-yellow tube, short greenish-white sepals and a striking dark red-purple corolla. The growth is upright and bushy with light green foliage, but the plant is quite slow-growing. It is reported to flower quite well in winter. Half hardy; Zones 9–10. Felix, Netherlands, 1987.

'Two Tiers'

The flowers of this cultivar develop in two stages, and are quite unlike those of other fuchsias. They are large doubles with a long thin pink tube, broad reflexed pink sepals and a pale beetroot-purple corolla. When the flowers are about 4–5 days old, four of the petaloids drop to a lower level, forming two tiers, hence the name. It has a lax bush growth habit with large mid-green foliage that is very suitable for hanging containers. Half hardy; Zones 9–10. Porter, UK, 1985.

'WALZ Tuba'

This is an unusual Dutch cultivar with strong upright growth, becoming quite tall, and therefore ideal as a standard. It has medium-sized to large dark green foliage and strikingly beautiful long flowers. The flowers are singles with a thin red tube 6cm (2½in) long, small red sepals tipped green and a small Tyrian-purple corolla. Grow it in a shady but light position for the best flower colours. Half hardy; Zones 9–10. Waldenmaier, Netherlands, 1987.

'Tarra Valley'

Encliandras

Encliandra hybrids have very small leaves and flowers, quite vigorous growth and are often among the last fuchsias to lose their leaves in winter. The name, from the Greek for 'enclosed male', refers to the fact that just four stamens protrude from the flower.

'Ariel'
This has slightly lax and self-branching growth, with tiny glossy dark green leaves. The tiny single flowers that freely appear in the leaf axils have a short cylindrical magenta tube, horizontal magenta sepals and a deep pink corolla. Eventually the fertilized flowers produce attractive round black berries 12mm (½in) in diameter. This fuchsia tolerates full sun when planted in the garden and is ideal trained as topiary, bonsai or other smaller shapes. Frost hardy; Zones 8–9. Travis, UK, 1973.

'Chapel Rossan'
This slightly lax-growing cultivar is a very pretty Encliandra with tiny distinctive flowers. They have a mid-pink tube and sepals, and a bright orange-red corolla. The small dark green leaves and wiry branches make it ideal for trained shapes, especially when grown as a ring. Frost hardy; Zones 8–9. Morris, UK, 1996.

'Cinnabarina'
This old cultivated form of *F.* x *bacillaris* is quite a vigorous grower, becoming untidy when grown in a greenhouse but making a compact bush in the border. The flowers are tiny singles with an orange tube, orange-red sepals and an orange corolla. The small leaves are mid-green. This is a good small hardy plant for rockeries and listed as being gall mite resistant. Hardy; Zones 7–8. Growth 45cm (18in). Raiser unknown, introduced *c*.1829.

'Ariel'

'Jiddles'
This is a vigorous hybrid with strong upright growth and small light green foliage. The tiny single flowers are self-coloured with a white tube, sepals and corolla that slowly age to a pale pink. Although the flowers are small, they stand out against the light green fern-like foliage. Half hardy; Zones 9–10. Iddles, UK, 1996.

'Lottie Hobby'
This old Encliandra hybrid with vigorous growth has wiry stems and mid-green leaves, and is slightly larger than most Encliandra cultivars. The small flowers have a tiny single light crimson tube, light crimson sepals and a light purple corolla. This

'Lottie Hobby'

fuchsia is ideal for growing topiary shapes because of its wiry self-branching growth, and is useful as a permanent outdoor planting in milder regions. Frost hardy; Zones 8–9. Edwards, UK, 1839.

'Marlies de Keijzer'
This cultivar is a cross between *F. encliandra* and *F. thymifolia* subsp. *thymifolia*. It has tiny single flowers with a red tube, sepals and corolla, which sit among the attractive tiny grey-green shiny foliage. The growth is slightly more compact than most Encliandra hybrids, probably due to the influence of *F. thymifolia* in its parentage. Half hardy; Zones 9–10. de Keijzer, Netherlands, 1999.

'Marlies de Keijzer'

'Miniature Jewels'

'Miniature Jewels'
This has trailing, self-branching growth with tiny serrated green leaves and can be trained in several ways. The flowers are tiny singles with a rose tube, rose-white sepals and a whitish-pink corolla. As the flower matures, the sepals and corolla turn dark pink, then red, creating a mixture of flower colours. Half hardy; Zones 9–10. Francesca, USA, 1976.

'Neopolitan'
This is a rather unusual Encliandra hybrid because the flowers can be red, pink or white, all growing at the same time, which creates a striking multicoloured effect. The typical flower is a tiny single, but is slightly larger than other Encliandra cultivars, with a red tube and sepals, and a pinkish-white corolla. The growth is very thin and wiry, with tiny mid- to dark green fern-like foliage. It is excellent as a topiary plant. Half hardy; Zones 9–10. Clark, UK, 1984.

'Oosje'
Hybridized from *F. parviflora* and *F. microphylla*, this is a vigorous grower and makes quite a large bush in a short time. It is very floriferous, with many tiny single flowers with a red tube maturing to crimson, red sepals held outwards also maturing to crimson and a red corolla turning dark red. The foliage is small and mid-green with the typical fern-like Encliandra appearance. It is an excellent choice for topiary work. Half hardy; Zones 9–10. van der Grijp, Netherlands, 1973.

'Radings Inge'
The fairly vigorous spreading growth of this fuchsia makes it useful in any kind of container, including hanging ones. It is very floriferous, with tiny single flowers with a red tube and sepals, and a pink-orange corolla. The small leaves are mid-green. Frost hardy; Zones 8–9. Reiman, Netherlands, 1980.

'Variegated Lottie Hobby'
A sport from 'Lottie Hobby', this fuchsia is reasonably vigorous and self-branching, with attractive tiny silver-cream and green foliage. It has a profusion of eye-catching flowers, which are tiny singles with a crimson tube, crimson sepals tipped pink and a crimson corolla. This plant is hardy in more sheltered areas. Frost hardy; Zones 8–9. Raiser and introduction date unknown.

'Waldfee'
This is a strong grower with rather matt mid-green foliage, large for an Encliandra. The flowers are tiny singles with a lilac-pink tube, lilac-pink sepals and a pale lilac-pink corolla. It forms a lax upright bush or, with persuasion, trails effectively when grown in a basket, and is also ideal for topiary. This plant is hardy in more sheltered areas. Frost hardy; Zones 8–9. Travis, UK, 1973.

'Oosje'

'Variegated Lottie Hobby'

Recent introductions

This section lists some of the newer cultivars that have been introduced by hybridizers and nurseries since 2005. They all have interesting characteristics and are well worth trying, but only time will tell if they become popular classics or fade into obscurity.

'Big White'
This new trailing Flemish cultivar has large double flowers with a white tube flushed mauve-rose, and long white sepals with a mauve-rose flush that are held downwards over a full white corolla. The medium-sized foliage is mid-green. It is good for baskets and mixed containers. Half hardy; Zones 9–10. Willems, Belgium, 2008.

'Black Country 21'
Named in honour of the 21st anniversary of the Black Country Fuchsia Society in the UK, this has small to medium-sized semi-erect single flowers with a deep pink tube, deep pink sepals and a plum-purple to aubergine corolla. The mid-green foliage is small to medium-sized. The growth is upright and bushy, but needs good pinching out to prevent it from making too much early tall growth. It is excellent as a pot plant, with some potential for a trained shape. Half hardy; Zones 9–10. Reynolds, UK, 2007.

'Brey'
One of the many recent European releases, this Flemish cultivar is rather unusual. The flower is a medium to large double with a long pale coral-rose tube, pale coral-rose sepals held horizontally with green tips and a full flared corolla whose petals are orange-red at the base and pale cyclamen-purple at the ends, veined with red. The plant is very free-flowering and its growth habit is a trailer with mid-green foliage. It should be very good in a basket on its own or in mixed baskets and containers. Half hardy; Zones 9–10. Michiels, Belgium, 2008.

'Cee-Jay-En'
This cultivar has upright and self-branching growth with medium-sized bright mid-green foliage. The medium

'Chris Bright'

to large single flowers have a cerise tube, cerise recurving sepals and a corolla that opens violet, is pink near the petal base and fades with maturity. It should be excellent for use as a larger pot plant and in containers, or you could try growing it as a half standard. Half hardy; Zones 9–10. Nicholls, UK, 2008.

'Chris Bright'
With an upright self-branching habit, this fuchsia has small single flowers with a pink tube, pink sepals held horizontally with recurving tips and a light powder-pink corolla with red anthers and a pink style. The small foliage has a mid- to dark green top surface. It is very suitable for growing in small pots and as a miniature or quarter standard. Half hardy; Zones 9–10. Fleming, UK, 2008.

'Daniel Reynolds'
This is an upright self-branching bush with a slightly spreading habit. It has small to medium-sized foliage that is mid- to dark green, and attractive small to medium-sized single flowers with a white tube, white sepals and a lavender-blue corolla. It flowers well and is suitable for smaller pots, miniature standards and smaller trained shapes. Take care not to overwater it, especially when young, because it is prone to botrytis. Half hardy; Zones 9–10. Reynolds, UK, 2005.

'Black Country 21'

'Daniel Reynolds'

'De Groot's Floriant'

Resulting from a species, *F. andrei*, crossed with the cultivar 'Fugi-san', this is an unusual upright shrub with medium to large mid- to dark green foliage. The medium-sized single flowers have a long red tube, short horizontal red sepals and a short orange corolla. The hardiness is unknown but it should probably be treated as tender. Tender; Zone 11. de Groot, Netherlands, 2007.

'Hastings'

Before being released, this cultivar was tested for three years in the area of Hartlepool, Cleveland, UK. It is a very pretty fuchsia, inheriting many characteristics from one of its parents, 'Sophie Louise'. It is a compact plant with small, narrow light green foliage and compact self-branching growth. The small single flowers have a very pale pink tube, pale pink to white sepals with a green tip and a pale lavender corolla. This fuchsia is excellent for small pots up to 13cm (5in) and also makes miniature standards and perhaps even a good bonsai. Half hardy; Zones 9–10. Riley, UK, 2008.

'Horsforth Dream'

With its upright but rather lax growth and medium-sized mid-green foliage, this fuchsia can be grown as a half standard or in hanging baskets, as a pot plant with

'Hastings'

cane supports, or in mixed containers. The medium-sized single flowers have a rose tube, horizontal rose sepals with green tips and a reddish-orange corolla. Half hardy; Zones 9–10. Swaby, UK, 2009.

'Jennifer Ann Porter'

This has a short-jointed upright self-branching bushy habit with attractive light to mid-green small foliage. The small single flowers have a pink tube, slightly recurving pink sepals and a white corolla with pink veining near the petal base. It has already been very successful in shows and is excellent for small pot sizes and smaller standards. This one is likely to be popular for some years. Half hardy; Zones 9–10. Reynolds, UK, 2005.

'Just Pilk'

This is an upright self-branching cultivar with small single flowers with a white tube, cream-white horizontal sepals blushed with pink underneath and a dusky pink corolla. The neat mid-green foliage complements the flowers well. It easily makes an attractive pot plant and will probably be successful trained as a smaller standard. Half hardy; Zones 9–10. Reynolds, UK, 2009.

'Kateric'

This floriferous new cultivar has very attractive medium-sized single flowers with a white tube, white sepals flushed with pink and a beautifully shaded pale violet corolla that matures to purple-pink. It has upright self-branching growth with medium-sized mid- to dark green foliage, makes a beautiful small pot plant and should grow well as a standard. Half hardy; Zones 9–10. Nicholls, UK, 2009.

'Jennifer Ann Porter'

'Just Pilk'

'Lynne Patricia'

'Maggie Rose'

'Lind'

This new German cultivar has a lax bush or stiff trailing manner of growth with medium-sized mid-green foliage. The large double flowers have a cream tube with pink blush, cream to pink horizontal sepals, darker pink underneath, and a full red corolla, flushed orange at the base. This fuchsia will do well in baskets or mixed containers, and might be worth trying as a weeping standard. Half hardy; Zones 9–10. Strümper, Germany, 2007.

'Lynne Patricia'

This has attractive medium-sized double flowers with a dark rose tube, sepals that are rose at the base, changing to white with green tips, and a white-flushed violet corolla with rose streaks. It has upright self-branching growth with medium-sized mid-green foliage, and is very suitable as a pot plant or for use in mixed containers. Half hardy; Zones 9–10. Swaby, UK, 2007.

'Maggie Rose'

This is a strong-growing bushy cultivar with medium-sized single flowers with a deep rose tube, long semi-reflexed deep rose sepals and a deep blue to violet corolla with the petals striped pink. The medium-sized foliage is an attractive shade of lime green. It is excellent as a pot plant, and should make a good standard. Half hardy; Zones 9–10. Waving, UK, 2006.

'My Little Gem'

This very pretty little cultivar from Gordon Reynolds, excellent in small pots, has small single flowers with a pale aubergine tube and sepals, and a corolla that opens dark purple and fades to aubergine. The flowers are held semi-erect off the small mid- to dark green foliage and the growth is small, self-branching and compact. This fuchsia is suitable for exhibition, and probably worth trying as a miniature standard. Half hardy; Zones 9–10. Reynolds, UK, 2008.

'Nicki Fenwick-Raven'

This new hybrid has tiny single flowers, although they are quite large for an Encliandra. The tube is long and greenish-white, and the sepals are white and recurved, but on ageing they mature to pink, then red. The corolla opens white but when mature becomes pink, edged with red. It is possible to see flowers of differing colours on the plant at the same time. The upright growth reaches 1–1.2m (3–4ft) high, with tiny fern-like, dark green foliage. Being an Encliandra, the plant may prove to be slightly more hardy than the present half hardy classification. Half hardy; Zones 9–10. Morrison, UK, 2008.

'Pippa Penny'

This very attractive new cultivar has lax bushy or stiff trailing growth with small mid-green foliage. The flowers are small singles with a white tube tinged with green, white sepals flushed pink with green tips and a corolla that opens pale violet, maturing to pale pink-violet. The corolla petals have a white blush at the base and an interesting, slightly ragged edge. It is suitable in small pots, small hanging pots or as standards, and perhaps as small trained shapes. Half hardy; Zones 9–10. Nicholls, UK, 2009.

'My Little Gem'

'Roselynne'

The lax bushy or stiff trailing growth of this fuchsia produces small single flowers with a short pale pink tube, pale pink sepals with green tips, darker pink underneath, and a pale lavender corolla with light reddish-purple streaks and white at the base. The appearance is enhanced by the oval mid-green foliage and the fat, round flower buds. It is good for growing in pots, hanging baskets and mixed containers, and perhaps for trained shapes. Half hardy; Zones 9–10. Swaby, UK, 2008.

'Suffolk Splendour'

This fuchsia was released in 2009 and was named in honour of the Stowmarket and District Flower Club's 50th anniversary in Suffolk, England. The large double flowers have a magenta tube, reflexed magenta sepals and a very full fluffy white corolla. It is an upright bushy plant, suitable for pots and large containers. Half hardy; Zones 9–10. Welch, UK, 2009.

'Toby Foreman'

This new upright self-branching floriferous cultivar makes a superb pot plant or standard. The flowers are medium-sized singles with a deep rose tube and sepals, and an attractive cream-white corolla.

'Vorarlberg'

The flowers stand out well against the neat mid-green foliage, making it a very striking plant. Half hardy; Zones 9–10. Waving, UK, 2007.

'Victorian Speed'

This is a new Flemish cultivar with a lax bushy or stiff trailing growth habit, with many large double flowers. The flowers have a rose tube with rose sepals hanging down that partially encircle the red and

purple petals of the full corolla. The foliage is slightly matt mid-green and its habit of growth makes it excellent to use in hanging baskets and containers, especially because it is so floriferous. Half hardy; Zones 9–10. Michiels, Belgium, 2008.

'Vorarlberg'

This trailing cultivar has medium-sized semi-double flowers with a pale pink tube, shell-pink sepals with yellow-green tips that are deeper pink underneath and a soft pink flared corolla. The growth is lax and trailing with mid- to dark green foliage, making it an interesting cultivar to grow in hanging containers or possibly as a weeping standard. Half hardy; Zones 9–10. Klemm, Austria, 2007.

'Widnes Wonder'

This distinctive new cultivar has profuse small single flowers with a white tube flushed pink, slightly recurving white sepals flushed pink and darker pink underneath, and a tight corolla that opens dark violet, maturing to purple-pink. It has small self-branching compact growth with neat mid-green foliage. It is excellent for small pots, and should be easy to grow as a small standard, the miniature type probably being the most suitable. Half hardy; Zones 9–10. Bright, UK, 2009.

'Toby Foreman'

'Widnes Wonder'

Index

'Maria Landy'

'Irene van Zoeren'

ACKNOWLEDGEMENTS

The publisher would like to thank Carol Gubler/ British Fuchsia Society for permission to take photographs at the BFS London Show.

The publisher would also like to thank the following for allowing their photographs to be reproduced in the book (t=top, b=bottom, l=left, r=right, m=middle).

Country, Farm and Garden: 83tr.
Tim Ellerby: 14tl, 17tr, 17b, 19tr, 44br, 47br, 53tl, 84br, 86b, 87t, 90tr, 91bl.
Manfried Kleinau: 20tr, 24t, 53b, 76t, 91t.
Rainer Klemm: 87bl.
John Nicholass: 12br, 16b, 18tr, 29b, 42tl, 46tr, 49bl, 49br, 69tr, 75tl, 77tl, 78br, 81t, 82b, 85b, 88t, 89t, 89bl, 89br, 90tl, 90b, 91br.
Photolibrary: 83b.
Henk Waldenmaier: 19tl.
Steven Wooster: 20b, 22br, 85tl.

Fuchsia colours and terms

The flower colours of fuchsias are widely described based on the Horticultural Colour Chart system developed by R.F. Wilson and published by the British Colour Council in collaboration with the Royal Horticultural Society in 1938, now long out of print. A reproduction of those colours commonly used in the descriptions in this book is set out in the grid below.

COLOURS

 carmine
 carmine-rose
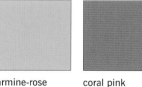 coral pink
 imperial-purple
 mallow-purple
 mauve
neyron-rose
orchid-purple
 rose-bengal
rose-madder
turkey-red
wisteria-blue

TERMS

Epiphytic: Describes plants that grow above the ground surface, using other plants or objects for support, but are not parasitic.
Paniculate: Describes a plant whose flowers are borne in clusters (panicles or racemes), and they often simultaneously include both flowers and fruit.
Pelargonium: Term used for all varieties formally commonly known as geranium, for example zonal geranium. The term 'geranium' now applies to the hardy variants such as the cranesbill.
Petaloids: Smaller petal-like structures within the corolla that can also be fused with other flower parts such as the stamens.
Raceme: An indeterminate (i.e. not terminated by a single flower) flowering stalk with a series of flowers on stalks branched from the main stem, with the oldest flowers at the base.
Self, or self-coloured: In which the tube, sepals and corolla of the flower are all the same or very similar colours.
Sub-raceme: A smaller flowering branch with fewer flowers than the main raceme.
Ternately: Arranged and growing in groups of three (of leaves).

Hardiness and zones

Plant entries in the directory of this book have been given hardiness descriptions and zone numbers. Other than plants listed as hardy, the hardiness descriptions are for plants grown in pots, while the zone numbers refer to plants in the ground.

HARDINESS

Tender: May be kept at a minimum temperature of 7°C (45°F).
Frost tender: May be damaged by temperatures below 5°C (41°F).
Half hardy: Can withstand temperatures down to 0°C (32°F).
Frost hardy: Can withstand temperatures down to -5°C (23°F).
Hardy: Can withstand temperatures down to -15°C (5°F).

ZONES

There is widespread use of the zone number system to express the hardiness of many plant species and cultivars. The zonal system used, shown here, was developed by the Agricultural Research Service of the United States Department of Agriculture. According to this system, there are 11 zones in total, based on the average annual minimum temperature in a particular geographical zone.

The zone rating for each plant indicates the coldest zone in which a correctly planted subject can survive the winter. Where a plant's hardiness is borderline, the first number indicates the marginal zone and the second the safer zone.

This is not a hard and fast system, but simply a rough indicator, as many factors other than temperature also play an important part where hardiness is concerned. These factors include altitude, wind exposure, proximity to water, soil type, the presence of snow or shade, night temperature, and the amount of water received by a plant. These kinds of factors can easily alter a plant's hardiness by as much as two zones. The presence of long-term snow cover in the winter especially can allow plants to survive in colder zones.

KEY TO ZONES
These maps show the zones in Europe and the USA. The temperature ranges apply worldwide.

	Zone 1	Below -45°C (-50°F)
	Zone 2	-45 to -40°C (-50 to -40°F)
	Zone 3	-40 to -34°C (-40 to -30°F)
	Zone 4	-34 to -29°C (-30 to -20°F)
	Zone 5	-29 to -23°C (-20 to -10°F)
	Zone 6	-23 to -18°C (-10 to 0°F)
	Zone 7	-18 to -12°C (0 to 10°F)
	Zone 8	-12 to -7°C (10 to 20°F)
	Zone 9	-7 to -1°C (20 to 30°F)
	Zone 10	-1 to 4°C (30 to 40°F)
	Zone 11	Above 4°C (40°F)

Birkenhead Park Station

Prior to electrification of its metals the Wirral Railway company used steam services of the Mersey Railway company at Birkenhead Park Station.

C000245204

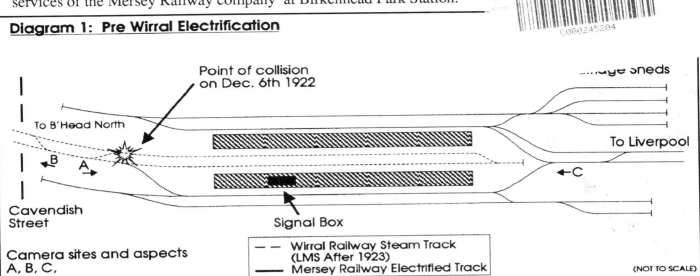

Diagram 1: Pre Wirral Electrification

Point of collision on Dec. 6th 1922

...uye sneds

To B'Head North

To Liverpool

B   A

C

Cavendish Street

Signal Box

Camera sites and aspects A, B, C,

— — Wirral Railway Steam Track (LMS After 1923)
——— Mersey Railway Electrified Track

(NOT TO SCALE)

A 1937 view looking towards West Kirby, with Park station behind the camera (point B), this scene has changed little over the years. The building to the left of the tunnel is the first purpose built Community Hall in the North of England, erected for the Trinity Church Parishioners although, a sign of the times, the windows have now been boarded up. In the right foreground can be seen coils of signal wire ready for use in the resignalling scheme. The gantry signals are LNWR semaphores which will have been used by the LMS to replace the original Wirral Railway signals. These are the inner home signals, one of which was missed by the driver of the steam train involved in the fatal accident on 6th December 1922. All the signals in this area have now been replaced by colour lights. The ends of the recently laid electric rails have been painted white to warn railway employees of this, then unfamiliar, hazard.

E.C. Lloyd Collection

Facing Park Station and looking West towards Birkenhead North (point C), the photographer is standing in the middle of the Mersey Railway electrified line! The locomotive, an LMS Fowler 2-6-2T, has moved off its train into the headshunt in order to run round the stock and take it back to West Kirby or New Brighton. New ballast has been laid in preparation for the new trackwork at this end of the station. On the left hand side, new point rodding and signal wire pulleys are evident. The Birkenhead Corporation bus shelter protrudes above Duke Street bridge parapet although for some strange reason, the top of the station buildings has been masked out during the development of the photographic negative.   *E.C. Lloyd Collection*

At 4.26pm on Wednesday 6th December 1922, a fatal accident occurred at Birkenhead Park Station. The 4.18 Park to West Kirby train was eight minutes late on leaving. Half the train had cleared the platform when the 4.00pm train from West Kirby, due to arrive in the same platform, passed signals at danger and collided with the departing train. Twelve passengers were taken to hospital with injuries to arms and legs after being thrown about compartments. The fatality occurred in the guard's van of the departing train. A Mrs. Margaret Wilson, the 68 year old invalid wife of a well known Liverpool solicitor, was returning to her home in Hoylake. Because she had to use a bath chair (a kind of 3 wheeled wicker basket chair) she had had to travel in the guard's van. The force of the collision catapulted her bath chair from one end of the van to the other with the result that she sustained a broken thigh and, subsequently, died of shock. The driver of the incoming train was 68 years of age and, after 40 years exemplary service, on this fateful night he misread the outer home signal in the misty dusk and failed to see the inner home signal at the tunnel mouth because it was obscured by the steam and smoke of the departing train. This was the first (and only?) fatal accident involving a passenger on the Wirral Railway which thus missed an historic accident free record by 25 days with the grouping into the LMSR becoming effective on 1st January 1923.
Ken Longbottom Collection

The subsequent electrification of Wirral's metals (then in LMS's ownership) resulted in significant changes in the track layout at Park Station as shown by the following diagrams:

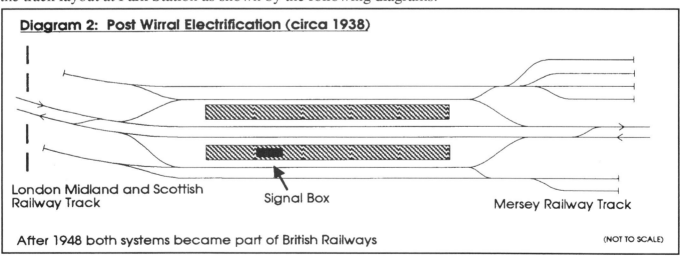

Diagram 2: Post Wirral Electrification (circa 1938)

London Midland and Scottish Railway Track

Signal Box

Mersey Railway Track

After 1948 both systems became part of British Railways

(NOT TO SCALE)

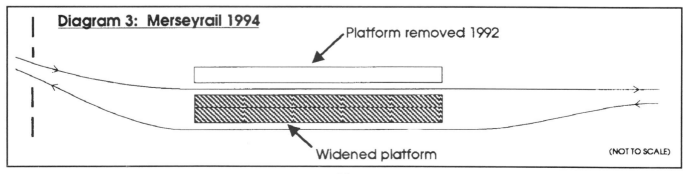

Diagram 3: Merseyrail 1994

Platform removed 1992

Widened platform

(NOT TO SCALE)

Birkenhead North looking west towards Bidston. The Wirral Railway manual signal box is still in use but the platform semaphore starting signal has now been replaced by a colour light positioned on the curve beyond the bridge. Opposite the curve and through the right hand bridge arch can be seen the corner of the maintenance and repair workshops of Birkenhead North Depot. The original Wirral Railway station was located to the right of this bridge and within the workshop site. The post-war platform lamps have now been replaced by tall vandal proof lights whilst the trackside wooden and wire mesh fences have been replaced by high security reinforced railings. This stretch of line has for a long time been noted as a repository for domestic and other rubbish. In the picture can be seen one pram (1960s large wheel type). Today's lineside tally could be considerably higher although a regular service of rubbish collecting trains is run as required.

E.C. Lloyd Collection

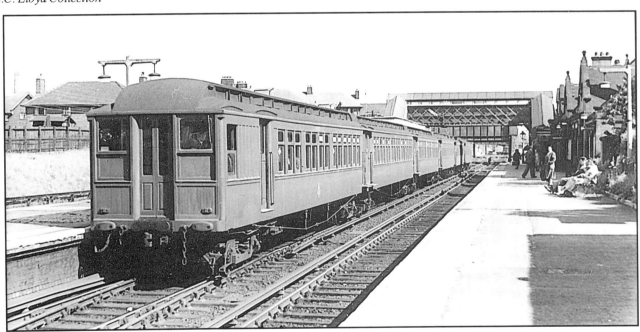

A 1954 view at Birkenhead North, originally named Birkenhead Dock (or was it Docks?) looking east towards Birkenhead Park and Liverpool. The distinctive former Mersey Railway Westinghouse stock had by this time acquired British Railways green livery and the logo of the time is just visible on the side of the last coach. The end for this stock came in 1956 when a further batch of units based on the original LMS design of 1938 (later known as class 503) entered service. The wooden footbridge with its passenger canopy had to be replaced with a metal footbridge for safety reasons in the late seventies. The starting signal for trains to Liverpool positioned on the overbridge was short of the platform end and this was later repositioned at the end of the platform.

N.R. Knight

Few local people will recognise this 1920s view of Bidston station with not a road or house in sight! The signal box and station buildings belonged to the Wirral Railway. The lamp man must have had a busy time attending daily to the platform and signal oil lamps. Beyond the tall station bracket signals, a train can just be seen on its way to West Kirby. A curious feature is that the relative heights of the station bracket signals indicate that the main line is not the Wirral Railway line to West Kirby but the Great Central connection branching away towards Chester and Wrexham. The Great Central's own lines are the left hand pair giving access to Bidston sidings and to the north end of the Birkenhead Dock estate. After the 1923 grouping, the Wirral Railway was taken over by the LMS and the Great Central became part of the LNER During the 1938 LMS electrification programme, the signal box and lower quadrant semaphore signals were replaced. However, the LMS could not touch the property of the LNER and the left hand group of signals remained in situ until the closure of Bidston sidings in the 1970s.
H.J. Leadbetter Collection

Bidston Station again facing West with the photographer standing in the middle of the down line!. LMS 0-4-4T 6405 is on a 'Sundays only' train from Birkenhead Woodside to Birkenhead Park in October 1937. This train will have travelled via Hooton and West Kirby, a journey of over 25 miles between two stations about a mile and a half apart as the crow flies! The previous photograph appears to have been taken from this wooden footbridge with its smoke deflectors. The bridge has long since been replaced by a concrete structure. The LNW steam set on the siding on the left is probably the stock of an excursion to New Brighton. That station had limited storage space and stock was often worked back to Bidston for stabling, the locomotive going on to Birkenhead North Shed for servicing. "Modernisation" signs are very evident. The ends of the conductor rails have been painted white to warn railwaymen and trespassers of the lethal hazard posed by the laying of the, then unfamiliar, electric rails. The platform edges have been replaced to meet the alignment of the recently introduced electric trains.
E.C. Lloyd Collection

RAILWAY STATIONS
of
WIRRAL
by Merseyside Railway History Group

Design & Origination:
Ian Boumphrey – Desk Top Publisher

Printed by:
Printfine Ltd.
Gibraltar Row Liverpool L3 7HJ
Tel: 0151 242 0000
Website: www.printfine.co.uk

Published by:
Ian & Marilyn Boumphrey
The Nook Acrefield Road Prenton Wirral CH42 8LD
Tel/Fax: 0151 608 7611
Website: www.yesterdayswirral.co.uk
For Merseyside Railway History Group

Reprinted : 2002

Copyright ©
All rights reserved. No part of this publication may be reproduced in any form without
prior permission from the authors

ISBN 1-899241-02-7

Front Cover: 1950s Poster [*Peter Jones collection*]

**PRICE
£6.95**

DEDICATION

This book is dedicated to the memory of former
Wirral Country Park Ranger
and a founder member of the Group,
Eric Jarvis.

PREFACE

History can be said to have started yesterday and in preparing this predominantly photographic survey the members of the MRHG, most of whom are passing (or have passed!) middle age, have tended to the longer and nostalgic view. Like their beloved steam locomotives, "cut-off" has been carefully considered and the illustrations predate the present generation of electric trains on Wirral, the 508 units, which are generally regarded as "modern" traction.

The summaries at the head of each chapter have been kept deliberately brief. There are many excellent publications available for those who, we hope, will wish to make further study of Wirral's fascinating railway past and a useful bibliography is included at the end of the book.

In 1981, the Group produced a booklet about the Hooton - West Kirby branch line** and the current review has brought this back sharply into focus. Whilst the Wirral Way must now count as a valuable asset to the community, as serious students of transport we must record our regret that the line has been lost. In transport terms, the retention and subsequent electrification of this line would have been investment in the future, especially in the light of what is now happening on the rest of the former Birkenhead Joint Lines. It is to be hoped that the potential for improvement and development of the former Great Central line through mid-Wirral is not similarly overlooked.

In considering Wirral's stations we would remind our readers that in the heyday of railways a railway station did not consist merely of a booking office, waiting rooms and platforms. Most stations had a goods warehouse, sidings, docks for the transhipment of special merchandise, coal merchants yards; all serving the needs of the local community.

Other features were individually styled signal boxes for controlling the movement of passing trains and access to and from the yards and sidings. Although no longer in railway use the remains of many of these buildings can still be seen, often converted for other uses so that many of to-day's passengers may not even be aware of their original purpose.

However, the attention of the readers is particularly drawn to the fact that the Autumn 1994 Wirral resignalling programme will entail the demolition of all the manually operated signal boxes, the replacement of semaphore signals by automatic colour lights and, in places, a transformation of the track layout.

It is hoped that this glimpse into the railway stations of Wirral will not only be a nostalgic trip for older readers, but will widen the horizon and sharpen the vision of younger readers about these vestiges of Wirral's railway transport past.

An appreciation of the past will hopefully develop a critical awareness of what is happening at the present with its consequences for the future of those who live and travel on the Wirral peninsula.

*"The Hooton to West Kirby Branch Line and the Wirral Way",

Published by the Metropolitan Borough of Wirral 1982.

ACKNOWLEDGEMENTS

We are indebted to the many photographers and organisations who have recorded the Wirral railway scene over the years, and who are credited under individual pictures. Particular thanks for their personal assistance and support are due to Neville Knight, Glyn Parry, John F.Ward, Bryan Wilson, David Goodwin and a former member of the Group, now resident in Yorkshire, Steve Weatherley.

INTRODUCTION

The ancient "Hundred of Wirral" is a peninsula about 15 miles long and from 6 to 7 miles wide, bounded on the west by the River Dee, on the east by the River Mersey and to the north by that part of the Irish Sea called Liverpool Bay.

At the beginning of the nineteenth century the peninsula had altered very little in appearance from what it had looked like when the Domesday Book was compiled in 1086, namely a few scattered hamlets and isolated settlements in an area comprising woodlands, stretches of heathland and patches of swamp.

Neither the establishment of a ferry terminal associated with the foundation of Birkenhead Priory in 1150, nor the conversion of the rough track through Wirral's woodlands into the Chester to Birkenhead turnpike road appear to have had any significant effect on the development of the peninsula. In 1811 the population of what is now central Birkenhead was 105.

In the eighteenth century Parkgate had been a major packet boat port for the crossing to Ireland, but at the dawn of the railway era, its importance had declined due to the silting of the River Dee.

From the mid-eighteenth century, Liverpool had steadily developed as the port serving the growth associated with Britain's Industrial Revolution, but the ability of Wirral to share in this economic progress was impeded by the problems of crossing a treacherous, fast flowing, tidal river at a time when the only means of transport depended on sails or oars.

The industrial, commercial and maritime development of the north eastern part of the Wirral peninsula dates from 1824 when John Laird decided to construct an ironworks in Birkenhead. This laid the foundation for one of the world's most famous shipbuilding yards. By 1841 the population of Birkenhead had risen to 8,000 and despite the introduction of steam propulsion on the Mersey ferries, the need for improved communications had become only too apparent to all concerned. The time of the Railway had arrived.

The map on the inside cover shows how the network of routes developed relatively quickly and eventually encompassed the peninsula. [This map is not to scale and in places has been deliberately distorted in order to show detail clearly].

OUR LOCAL EXPRESS
Seacombe to West Kirby

Chapter One
THE RAILWAY COMES to WIRRAL

Development of the Chester to Birkenhead Railway

During the 1830s George Stephenson had planned a line from Chester to Birkenhead with a terminus at Grange Lane adjacent to what later became Town Station. This location was not chosen for the benefit of the travelling public but to satisfy the conflicting interests of the local ferry operators at Woodside, Monks Ferry and Tranmere. Grange Lane was equidistant from these three ferries thus favouring none of them. Intermediate stations were built at Bebington, Hooton, Sutton (later Ledsham) and Mollington.

Despite the success of the Liverpool and Manchester Railway, which had been operating since 1830, the news about the relative merits of speed and safety of contemporary road and rail transport, had obviously not reached quite a few of the inhabitants of the peninsula . On the opening day of the Birkenhead & Chester Railway, a race was arranged to establish the relative merits of these competing forms of transport. A stage coach, drawn by a four horse team left the Woodside Hotel and sped along the Chester road at the same time as a steam hauled train departed from Grange Lane station along the single line track to Chester. After arrival at Chester, the train passengers were able to ask their opposite numbers in the stage coach, "What took you so long?", thereby resolving the public debate once and for all. It is worthy of note that the Birkenhead line was in use ahead of the line from Crewe to Chester.

Monks Ferry, which had nothing to do with the Priory, was promoted by the Bryan Family and opened, without authority, in April 1838. Following proceedings instituted by the operators of the Woodside ferry, they were compelled to close the ferry early in 1840. The railway company, arguing that a ferry for the exclusive use of railway passengers was not a public ferry, purchased Monks Ferry and an extension of the line from Grange Lane to the Ferry was opened on 23rd October 1844. Quite clearly, the promoters of the Birkenhead & Chester Railway were not greatly concerned with Birkenhead but with traffic to and from Liverpool.

In 1847, the line to Chester was doubled in order to deal with the ever increasing traffic, especially after the opening of the Birkenhead Docks. These docks steadily developed into a complex of quays with a frontage of ten miles and was virtually dependent on rail transport until the post war growth of road haulage particularly in the 1960s and 1970s.

Just beyond the confines of the Hundred of Wirral, other railway developments were taking place. The Lancashire & Cheshire Junction Railway was formed in order to build a line from Chester through Helsby to connect with the London & North Western Railway at Warrington. The Lancashire & Cheshire Junction, whose line was then only in the early stages of construction, absorbed the Birkenhead & Chester in 1847.

The new company, which was called the Birkenhead, Lancashire and Cheshire Junction Railway Company, was too short of funds to effect any significant improvements on the Birkenhead - Chester line.

Whilst all this had been going on, the Great Western Railway was approaching Wirral from the South West culminating in its absorbtion of the Shrewsbury and Chester Railway in 1854. The Great Western Railway was also an active supporter of the Birkenhead, Lancashire & Cheshire Junction Railway through which it hoped to obtain an outlet to the Mersey. The London & North Western was equally anxious to keep it out, but eventually the two major companies were forced to compromise and the BL&CJ was taken over by the Great Western and London & North Western jointly on 20th November 1860 and became known thereafter as the Birkenhead Joint Railway.

The new company now had far greater resources available for improvements. Rock Ferry station was opened in 1862 and the "glory hole" station at Monks Ferry was closed to passengers on 1st April 1878 with the simultaneous opening of a main line terminus worthy of the name at Woodside.

In 1863, the Joint Company constructed a branch from Hooton to Helsby for the movement of freight between Birkenhead docks and the London and North Western Railway's main lines at Warrington and Manchester, without having to pass through the busy and congested junctions at Chester. Passenger traffic on this stretch of line was purely local with two stations within the Wirral boundaries - Sutton (later Little Sutton) and Whitby Locks (later Ellesmere Port).

In 1866, the branch line from Hooton to Parkgate was opened with intermediate stations provided at Hadlow Road (Willaston) and Neston. This line was originally intended to tap the coal traffic from the Colliery at Neston. It was not until 1886 that further development took place with an extension to West Kirby. This project entailed the replacement of the station at Parkgate and the construction of intermediate stations at Heswall (1886), Thurstaston (1886), Kirby Park (1894) and Caldy (1909).

In response to traffic demands, the main line was quadrupled from Ledsham Junction to Green Lane, Birkenhead in the period 1902-08, thereby segregating slow freight traffic from the passenger services. This measure entailed the enlargement and reconstruction of the passenger stations and today's remains and artifacts on this stretch of line date mainly from this period.

From 1878 until 1967 Birkenhead possessed a splendid terminal station at Woodside of respectable proportions with a train shed covering much of the platforms. The original booking hall was, in fact, alongside the Graving Dock on the south side of the station and was used for most of it's life as a parcels depot, thus earning the station the unique distinction of being "the wrong was round". There were two main causes for this unhappy fate for an otherwise finely planned station. Firstly, the railway's original scheme for a covered approach direct to the ferry was baulked by the ferry authorities. Then, in 1901, the Corporation laid out their new tram terminus adjacent to the "back door" and it became apparent that, to meet the public needs, "reversal" of the station would have to become permanent.

A 1954 view of the "front" entrance with its fine port-cochere. The two parcels vans are an indication of the reduced status of this part of the station - far removed from its intended use of covering the gentry as they alighted from their carriages.

G.D. Hawkins

A view of the splendid , but little used as such, booking hall entered directly from the port-cochere. Described by one commentator as "Victorian baronial", excellent brickwork with stone features and dressing is evident, the whole being spanned by a magnificent hammer beam trussed roof. It is also recorded that the building had exceptional fireplaces, but the prospect of heating this place would have surely made greater demands on the companies' coal stocks than any of their locomotives!

Stan Roberts

6

A view of the original rear entrance to Woodside which became the principal entrance for a large part of the station's life. Many arriving passengers booked their tickets at the "temporary" booking office on the concourse and remained unaware of the suite of waiting and refreshment rooms adjacent to the piles of parcels in the original hall. Birkenhead townsmen were said to complain that their station had a "Mary Ann front and a Queen Anne back" and as late as 1954 the local press were petitioning BR to provide an entrance "befitting a terminus station of no little standing". The benefit of integrated transport is evidenced by a bus on route 40 to Eastham awaiting departure close to the station entrance. Birkenhead Corporation's fleet of buses was an outstanding municipal undertaking and their fine latter day livery of blue and cream is remembered with affection by many. Beyond this bus is one of the equally well known Crosville buses which ran to all parts of Wirral. *L&GRP Collection, courtesy National Railway Museum, York*

A 1950s interior view showing some of the fine structural features - graceful wrought iron columns and a splendid essay in decorative brickwork on the rear wall. The replacement timber booking hall, following the demise of the original booking hall, can be seen on the platform concourse. The former joint ownership is still evident with ex-LMSR coaching stock on the left and chocolate and cream liveried ex-GWR stock on the right. In it's heyday this station employed a stationmaster, three inspectors and 75 staff and there were 163 trains a day to be dealt with including

the empty stock movements to Blackpool Street sidings. The narrow confines of the station throat and a rising gradient of 1 in 95 in Chester Street tunnel compounded the operational difficulties. As an example of the importance of the Station, Railway Clearing House figures for 1913 showed ticket bookings for 425,965 passengers. This figure does not include the 150 annual contract ticket holders who used the railway and then the ferry to travel to Liverpool daily. The clock overlooking the platforms on the right of the picture was of a type often found on main line stations and was made by Joyce of Whitchurch. There appears to be a space for a similar clock on the left hand side although none was ever fitted. *L&GRP Collection, courtesy National Railway Museum, York*

A 1930s view from the platform ends which shows the Rose Brae bridge which was demolished when the graving dock was extended in 1961. Removal of this bridge opened up the view of the station train shed and enabled its fine proportions to be more easily appreciated. The engine nearest the camera, an ex-LNWR 'Coal Tank' is the 'Station Pilot' identified as such by the position of the lamp on the buffer beam. The Station Pilot was used for moving stock in and out of the platforms. Beyond it are two unidentified GWR locomotives. The first, carrying Express Passenger headlamps, is at the head of a train ready to depart. The second locomotive is on the middle road used for releasing engines once they have brought a train into the terminus. However, the tender is piled high with coal and is more in keeping with an engine about to take a train out rather than just having brought one in.
A.G. Coltas

A coal train passing through Monks' Ferry station on route to the quayside. It is hauled by a locomotive with a distinctive history. Designed and built by Kitsons of Leeds as a "tram" engine, it was first used on the West Lancashire Railway on their Southport - Crossens service but proved to be too light for the task. It was sold to the Liverpool Overhead Railway and served for many years in their engineers department where it's duties included de-icing in winter. Although never officially named, it was always known as "Lively Polly".
K. Longbottom Collection

Two views of the remains of Monks' Ferry station. The first, dating from 1954, shows the form of the roof structure which had been removed by the time of the later picture which dates from 1958. The former station area was used as a permanent way engineers depot and the quayside by the Monks' Ferry Steam Coal Co. for servicing of the once ubiquitous Mersey tug-boats. Thus, despite it's closure to passengers as early as 1878, the branch survived until 1967. The lower view shows one of the Monk's Ferry Steam Coal Co.'s unusual wagons which comprised three separate containers for easy discharge into the bunkers of the ships. This was an early example of containerisation; the wagons dating back to the early years of the century. The white building overlooking the station is Perry's ship and yacht chandlers and, for a change, a local firm still in business.
Both:J.A. Peden

Birkenhead Town station entrance was an unimpressive affair situated in the commercial part of the town. Consisting of red brick with stone dressing, similar in architectural style to the entrance to Rock Ferry station, this building, replacing the earlier structure was probably included in the "modernisation and upgrading" programme carried out during the quadrupling of the tracks in the early years of the present century. The proportions of the clerestory light might give the impression to the casual visitor that the building was a municipal bath house rather than a railway station booking hall. The construction and opening of the Mersey road tunnel, which was opposite the station entrance, left the station virtually cut off from reasonable access to the market area and to the residential district by Birkenhead Priory. This situation led to the closure of the station in 1945.   *K. Longbottom Collection*

A rare view of the former Birkenhead Town station, looking towards Woodside which was approached by a sulphurous tunnel under Chester Street. Important stages in the development of Birkenhead's main line railway can be gleaned from this view. To the left and behind the workshop buildings was the original Grange Lane terminus of the Birkenhead and Chester Railway opened in 1840 and closed in 1844. To the right of the platform fence and passing into the tunnel which is just visible, was the line to Monks' Ferry which was Birkenhead's second terminal until replaced by Woodside in 1878. Not all trains stopped here and train spotters used the ramp (seen in the centre of the picture above the signal box) for viewing to save buying a platform ticket at Woodside.

E.C. Lloyd Collection

The impressive span of tracks seen in this view conveys some idea of Birkenhead's former importance as a railway centre. This is Green Lane junction where the lines to the Docks and the Shipyard branched from the passenger line to Woodside. It is also close to the site of Lime Kiln Lane Station. Lime Kiln Lane later became St. Paul's Road and the station name was changed to Tranmere about 1855. This station closed a few years later and no photographs have been traced. In this view, former GWR locomotives are in charge of the freight trains whilst, on the passenger working, the joint line tradition of one company's locomotive hauling the other company's stock is maintained with a former LMSR Stanier Mogul 2-6-0 hauling ex-GWR coaches. The massive structure which can be seen behind the bracket signal is the concrete coaling stage at Mollington Street locomotive depot. This equipment enabled a complete wagon load of coal to be hoisted up and tipped into a locomotive tender. This coaling stage had a very short life, being built as late as 1955 and then demolished in 1967.

J.A. Peden

A Paddington to Birkenhead train, carrying express headlamp code, pauses at Rock Ferry. The 'temporary' nature of the numberplate and shed code on the smoke box door of this Caprotti geared BR standard class 5 locomotive is symptomatic of the mid-1960s when steam traction was nearing its demise. This picture gives some idea of the scale of Rock Ferry station in its heyday with an extensive footbridge spanning all six platforms. The towers contained goods lifts.

B. Taylor

This photograph shows one of four special trains chartered by Lever Bros. Ltd at Bebington Station on Friday 25th May 1900. The train is hauled by a GWR Armstrong Goods 0-6-0 (Possibly No 794 built in 1873) leading a tender engine of unknown identity which has a wheel arrangement of either 2-4-0 or 4-4-0. The leading engine is carrying a headboard 'Lever Bros. Port Sunlight - Paris'. On this occasion the trains took the employees travelling to Paris for the 1900 Universal Exhibition and most of the work-force went on the trip. Excursions of this nature also took place in 1905 to Brussels and in 1910 to the Brussels Exhibition and are part of the folklore of Port Sunlight's heritage. Some readers may not be aware that a paternal attitude towards employees is not something uniquely Japanese. In fact, in Britain during the Edwardian era several firms such as Rowntrees, Cadbury and Bass arranged railway excursions for their workers as well as Lever Bros.
Lever Bros. Heritage Centre

An undated view of Bebington station looking towards Port Sunlight and Chester. New Ferry had been added to the station's title in 1895. The facilities provided on the island platform are clearly spartan and some repair work appears to be in hand. The signals for both lines are "pulled off" and it is suspected that at this time the local signal box was "switched out" pending formal closure and removal. The lower distant signals are "on" thereby warning drivers to reduce speed because the next stop signals, located at Port Sunlight, are also "on" ie. in the "stop" position.
Lens of Sutton

A 1967 view at Bebington looking towards Rock Ferry with the nearby signalbox still in operation. At this time each station on the line still had it's own working box and there were several locations which still boasted LNWR signals, although those illustrated here are LMS upper quadrant pattern.
H.B.Priestley/Pacer Archives

Surprisingly, despite the proximity of the Lever factory complex to the Birkenhead and Chester line, Port Sunlight did not have a station until 1914. At first this was just a halt of wooden construction intended for the private use of the factory employees in the morning and the evening. Later on the station was enlarged and a subway built, but it was not until 1927 that the public were given full access to the railway services. The wooden platforms built in 1927 survived until 1969 when they and much of the station were rebuilt. In this picture, taken in 1957, the 6.13pm Birkenhead to Helsby, headed by 2-6-4 tank No.42599 enters the up platform. The LMS type 'Hawks-eye' name board and the wooden waiting shelter are clearly seen.

H.B. Priestley/Pacer Archives

A view, looking towards Chester, of the unusual arrangements at Port Sunlight when the line was still quadrupled. Platforms were provided on the Up fast and Down slow lines only, which must have occasionally negated the benefits of the segregated tracks. Both platform buildings and the main administration block, which still stands today, were of an individual design presumably to blend with the village.
Peter E. Baughan

An early view of Spital Station looking in the direction of Birkenhead. The main building is a splendid structure in Italianate style and had a very short life, being demolished to make way for the quadrupling of the tracks as far as Ledsham in 1907/8. Note the distinctive enamel advertising signs for Sunlight Soap and Tennants Lager.
Courtesy Bebington Central Library

Another view of Spital looking in the other direction and showing a rustic setting with ivy-clad waiting shelter and the squat signal box of the early joint line design. One of these boxes survived at Upton-by-Chester until the 1960s. The signals are standard LNWR pattern.
Courtesy Bebington Central Library

At the time of the quadrupling, Spital station was completely rebuilt and these two views show the new arrangements. This picture, looking towards Chester, shows the booking office and substantial footbridge. The signal box with its distinctive 'look-out' extension can be seen beyond the bridge.
H.B. Priestley/Pacer Archives

In this view of Spital Station, looking towards Birkenhead in 1958, 2-6-2 tank No.40209 is arriving on the 10.05 Birkenhead-Llandudno train.
H.B. Priestley/Pacer Archives

A general view, looking towards Chester, of the principal buildings at Bromborough taken in 1961. The lines to the left of the picture are a result of the quadrupling in 1907/8. The roof of the original station building alongside the old lines can be seen towering above the footbridge to the right of the picture whilst the small goods shed, remains of which still survived at the time of writing, can be seen under the right hand arch of the bridge. The majority of trains to Birkenhead would use the slow line platforms on the right and this is evidenced by the superior waiting facilities provided by the canopy and waiting rooms.
R.M. Casserley

Bromborough again, this time viewed from the Chester side of the bridge with ex-LMSR 2-6-4T No.42570 passing on the up slow line. The former station building can be more clearly seen on the left of the picture. The line coming towards the photographer led to the station yard and the goods warehouse which is just visible in the previous photograph. *H.B. Priestley/Pacer Archives*

The former joint line station building, seen here from the station approach, still survives in use at Hooton. The covered footbridge is of later LNWR design. This station originally had no less than six through platforms and a bay, those furthest from the main building serving the former branch line to West Kirby, pictured elsewhere in this book. The bay, used for trains to Ellesmere Port and Helsby, was located just behind the white building. For such a large and busy station, the entrance was unpretentious and not readily apparent to passengers approaching the station.

E.C. Lloyd Collection

The signal boxes and signalling equipment on the joint line were predominantly of LNWR construction and their signals were described by railway historian George Dow as "elephantine". They dominate this view of Hooton Station taken in it's heyday as a busy double junction. To assist drivers, signals applicable to slow or goods lines were fitted with rings which were removed by the LMSR following the grouping of 1923. The building to the right of the picture beyond the line of goods wagons was in use in the early days as a locomotive shed. The tall chimney was at the Tragasol Products Ltd works with the Wirral Cattle Mart adjacent to it. On the opposite side of the tracks from the works was an extensive cattle dock which was used as a watering place for cattle in transit and also for washing out cattle vans. Smells from both of these line-side features could permeate the station area to the discomfort of waiting passengers when the wind was in the "wrong" direction.

John Ryan Collection

16

A Chester bound express is leaving Hooton under clear signals. The train is hauled by a GWR "Barnum" class 2-4-0 mixed traffic locomotive. GWR locomotive enthusiasts will note that this is one of the later examples of this class, earlier ones had the dome further forward on the first ring of the boiler and the front springs below the axleboxes. The train is probably bound for Paddington consisting as it does of a lengthy rake of GWR corridor stock. At Chester, where the train will reverse direction, a more powerful locomotive will take over for the journey onward.
E.C. Lloyd Collection

As mentioned earlier, it was usual on joint line services for locomotives of one company to haul the stock of the other, as seen here where an ex-LNWR 2-4-2T is hauling a fixed rake of GWR suburban stock clearly marked as Set No.7 of the Chester Division. The train is leaving Hooton from the Ellesmere Port Bay whilst a train from Birkenhead can just be seen under the bridge arriving at the main platform.
E.C. Lloyd Collection

This view of the four platform Ledsham station shows the substantial passenger facilities provided. In fact, the station never achieved the commercial potential envisaged by the Joint Company simply because the surrounding area remained rural. The residential development of the neighbourhood is only now beginning to occur, nearly twenty years after the station closed. The prominent LNWR signals had to give the driver of an approaching train a clear sighting despite the restricted view imposed by the station buildings and overbridge.
Ian Boumphrey Collection

A view at Ledsham taken after closure but with the station buildings still intact. This was the last station on the quadrupled section from Rock Ferry and just beyond here the lines converged at Ledsham Junction signal box for the double line section to Mollington and Chester. The signal in the photograph is the distant signal for Ledsham Junction.
Peter E. Baughan

A 1930s view of a GWR mixed freight train bound for Pontypool Road passing Capenhurst hauled by 2-6-2T No.5160 which would probably only work the train as far as Chester. Mogul or Hall class locomotives were normally used on this train.
E.C. Lloyd Collection

A 1961 view of the main station building at Capenhurst which was situated on the Up (Chester-bound) platform. It is interesting to compare this with the previous view; the much reduced foliage and the presence of the motor car being consistent with the march of urbanisation. Regrettably the present day station is almost reduced to an industrialised setting.
R.M. Casserley

A period view of Hadlow Road station with the staff posing on the platform. The signalman, however, has a duty to perform and is waiting in the space between the tracks, known to railwaymen as the "six-foot", in order to collect the train staff for single line working, from a goods train arriving in the loop from the Hooton direction.
H.J. Leadbetter Collection

Another view of the station building taken in 1964 and showing how little the scene had changed. Even the distinctive gas lamp on the corner of the building had survived. Readers may care to make comparisons with the modern day scene when next they walk the "Wirral Way".
H.J. Leadbetter

The crossing gates at Hadlow Road were exceptionally long because of the oblique angle at which the road crossed the railway. They were not worked from the signal box and it is presumed that the gateman "resided" in the brick cabin, complete with fireplace and chimney, on the left of the picture.
H.J. Leadbetter Collection

The substantial waiting shelter on the West Kirby bound platform was built in red flemish bond brickwork. There was an identical structure at Thurstaston and it is suspected that both date from the extension of the line from Parkgate in 1886.
H.J. Leadbetter

A view of Neston station taken after British Railways had renamed it Neston South to avoid confusion with the station on the Mid Wirral line which was renamed Neston North. One wonders how the passengers had coped for the previous half century and more! The main building is the original Joint Line design and is somewhat similar to Hadlow Road. The hut in the foreground is probably a later addition, being one of the LNWR's standard designs. A curiosity is the bay window in the station master's house in what on assumes was the main bedroom. *David Lawrence /Courtesy Hugh Davies*

A view at Parkgate of the platform for Hooton bound trains taken from a train en route to West Kirby. The buildings were a modification of the LNWR standard timber modular design with a tiled roof and red brick chimneys, contrasting with their more usual slate and blue or yellow brick styles. Two unusual features were the signal box, which was incorporated into the building on the West Kirby side, presenting a "bay window" appearance projecting from the last panel and the provision of a passenger subway between the platforms. This latter feature was normally only found at more "urban" locations. This station is sited on the "new" alignment to West Kirby following the extension of the line in 1886. No photographs of the original station have been traced but it is presumed to have been in a similar architectural style to it's neighbours at Neston and Hadlow Road. The site of the former station was developed as a goods yard and remained in use until closure of the line. Vehicles using this yard can just be sighted beyond the signal in this view. The principal user of the yard in it's latter days was a local waste oil contractor for tanker traffic.

David Lawrence /Courtesy Hugh Davies

22

A delightful Edwardian view of the passing station at Heswall on the Hooton to West Kirby branch. The signalman steps out briskly from his cabin with the train staff for the single line to Parkgate. The train comprises a rake of short wheelbase coaches, probably in the splendid "plum and spilt milk" livery of the LNWR and is hauled by one of their Webb tank engines. The neat and tidy appearance of the station gardens will be noted. Possibly this is the work of the signalman who appears to be propagating plants in his signal box.   *E.C. Lloyd Collection*

A 1950s view of a train entering Heswall station from West Kirby hauled by an ex- LMSR Stanier designed 2-6-2T locomotive, whose smokebox numberplate is indistinguishable. It is unfortunate that the unusual booking hall has been "cropped" in this view. The station clock was a well-known local feature, being maintained "right time" long after closure of the passenger service, presumably by the signalman. Ironically, there have been some views published of diesel multiple units in this station, when they were employed for driver training duties prior to their introduction on the mid-Wirral line in 1960.   *David Lawrence/Courtesy Hugh Davies*

A view of the main station building at Thurstaston. Originally it boasted a canopy of similar design to those at Heswall. The squat signal box is of the LNWR standard Type 4 design and again is comparable with Heswall. The single line working was by means of the Webb-Thompson train staff system, whereby a specially grooved metal bar was released electrically to permit passage of trains between the respective "passing loops". The staff, which was more cumbersome than the later electric "token", was carried on the engine between signalboxes. Notwithstanding this normally foolproof system, a collision occurred between two freight trains at Thurstaston in 1957, causing minor damage to the loop platform on the opposite side to this view. *David Lawrence*

In this view of a train about to depart for West Kirby, the exchange of staffs between the signalman and the engineman is more clearly demonstrated. This 1954 view also shows the continuing joint line tradition with a former LMSR engine No.40101 hauling stock of Great Western origin. *N.R. Knight*

Caldy station, opened in 1909, was a simple design with only a single wooden platform. The basic corrugated iron building, enhanced by decorative barge boards on the gable ends, comprised ticket office, waiting room and toilet. The upper picture, dating from 1951, shows an early Saturday morning train from West Kirby. The sole passenger is believed to be bound for Mostyn House school at Parkgate in the days when Saturday morning attendance at such establishments was the norm! In the lower picture, taken after the station's closure in 1954, a Hooton bound train hauled by LMS 2-6-2T (No.40101) is passing through the station. Although the station had closed earlier in the year, the photographer had managed to retrieve the signboard from the grass in order to complete his picture.
Above: J.N. Barlow Collection
Below: NR Knight

The simplistic nature of Kirby Park station is evident in this view which was actually taken a month after its closure. The coal siding just visible in the foreground remained in use until the final closure of the line in 1962.
N.R. Knight

This view towards Thurstaston shows the coal siding a little more clearly as well as the provision made for doubling the line when constructing all the overbridges. On this occasion a former Great Western engine is paired with LMSR stock.
N.R. Knight

This train has arrived at the West Kirby terminus of the joint GW/LNW Railway line from Hooton. It is an ex-GWR auto (push & pull) train comprising 0-4-2T Loco No.1457 and coach which had a driving facility at in the end compartment. Such trains were the successors to railmotors such as that illustrated on page 62 (Neston & Parkgate) with the advantage of additional power. The children appear to be a party of school boys, accompanied by two nuns. It is interesting to compare this picture (taken in 1954) with the view taken at Moreton in the 1920s (Page 36). Whilst the elaborate headgear of the nuns has gone unchanged for three decades, most of the boys seem to have dispensed with theirs!
The late H.C. Casserley/courtesy R.M. Casserley

A view in the opposite direction showing the same train which had arrived as the 2.50pm ex-Hooton and has moved back towards Grange Road to take water. The stock yard of the former Wirral Timber Co. adjoins the approach road through the goods yard on the right of the picture. A small turntable was originally situated in the depression in the grass embankment adjacent to the bridge abutment on the other side of the line. The road bridge has been removed and the site of the timber yard is now a road junction adjacent to the West Kirby Concourse.
The late H.C. Casserley/courtesy R.M. Casserley

The line from Hooton to Helsby was opened in 1863 and boasted neat Jacobean style buildings built from red Cheshire sandstone. The first stop after Hooton was Little Sutton seen in the upper picture in LNWR days with distinctive gas lamps and a fine station garden. A second picture, dating from 1974, shows a footbridge added and the original gas lamps replaced by modern electric lights. The ivy has also disappeared from the station building. In more recent times the station's principal claim to fame was the longevity of the signalman, Joe Ellams, who was still in active service on his eightieth birthday.

Upper: E.C. Lloyd Collection
Lower: Stan Roberts

This simple waiting shelter on the Hooton bound platform at Little Sutton is a splendid portrayal of the stonemason's art, sporting feature copings and ball and spike finials. It is believed that this was originally an "open" shelter and that the timber and glass frontage was added later.
Stan Roberts

The station building at Ellesmere Port was slightly larger than it's once country neighbours on either side with curved Dutch pediments to the gable walls. This 1950s view looking towards Hooton shows the arrangement before the level crossing was replaced by an overbridge to relieve what had become a major problem to the town's traffic flow. No. 2 Signalbox, seen just beyond the crossing, controlled the junction for the Manchester Ship Canal Co.'s lines to Eastham which in the heyday of rail-borne freight added to the intensity of traffic through the station.

H.B. Priestley/Pacer Archives

A contrasting Edwardian view showing a train of 4 wheelers hauled by a LNW 2-4-2 tank entering the station past the original squat signal box. The passengers on the platform form an interesting cross section of Edwardian society. The variety of general merchandise being handled at this station is also worthy of scrutiny. Beyond the station buildings can be seen the locomotive shed, latterly used by the Manchester Ship Canal Company's locomotives.

Ian Boumphrey Collection

Prior to the construction of Stanlow oil terminal and refinery, Ince & Elton was the most remote and truly rural station in the area. It was situated between the small villages bearing these names and, to the east, marshland covered the whole area between the railway lines and the Manchester Ship Canal all the way to Frodsham and the River Weaver. In subsequent years the oil refinery was the major source of freight over the line. An ex-LMS 2-8-0 No.48017 heads a tanker train through Ince & Elton in 1962. The station buildings are of the same design as Little Sutton.

H.B. Priestley/Pacer Archives

Chapter Two
THE WIRRAL RAILWAY

The Hoylake Railway was a grand scheme to link Seacombe and Birkenhead with Hoylake, New Brighton and Parkgate. In the event, only the Birkenhead to Hoylake section was built initially and opened in 1866 with intermediate stations at Bidston, Moreton and Meols. The line lasted only a short time and failed through lack of traffic. This was scarcely surprising as at that time most of the line passed through sparsely populated and marshy countryside.

In 1869 or 1870, depending on which historian you consult, bailiffs took over the line on behalf of a local landowner who had not been paid for the land which he had sold to the Railway Company.

In 1872 the Hoylake and Birkenhead Rail and Tramway Company took over the concern and reopened the section between Leasowe and Birkenhead which had been closed by the bailiffs. This company extended the single line to West Kirby in 1878 and into a new station named Birkenhead Dock (or Docks, depending on which official document you are consulting) later to be re-named Birkenhead North. In 1881 the name of the company was changed to the Seacombe, Hoylake and Deeside Railway.

By 1888 the branch to New Brighton was built. In the same year a new company, known as the Wirral Railway, constructed a stretch of line to connect the Seacombe, Hoylake & Deeside Railway Station at Birkenhead Dock with the Mersey Railway station at Birkenhead Park. Finally, in 1891, the two companies were amalgamated under the banner of the Wirral company to promote and develop the entire network.

Increased resources soon produced results including the opening of a proper station at Leasowe crossing in 1894 together with the completion of the branch from Bidston to Seacombe with an intermediate station at Liscard and Poulton. In 1896 West Kirby station was rebuilt and the line from Hoylake doubled. In 1907, a station was opened at Leasowe Road (Wallasey Village). In short, the Wirral Railway attained all the original objectives except that, as mentioned in the previous chapter, the connection to Parkgate had been pre-empted by the Birkenhead Joint Company's branch from Hooton to West Kirby.

The third rail electrification of the Wirral lines by the LMS, completed in 1938 aroused considerable interest. At Birkenhead Park, where the Wirral lines had an end-on junction with the (already electrified) Mersey Railway, the station buildings remained unaltered but considerable changes were made to the track layout and signalling. In this view of Park Station, taken at point A on the diagram looking East towards Liverpool, the separation of the centre steam lines (Wirral) and four rail electric system of the Mersey Railway on the right is clearly seen. The signal box is on the platform behind the water column. On the left hand side, permanent way materials are stacked in preparation for the track alterations. The new signal at the far left has a cross on the signal arm to indicate that it is not yet in use. A Mersey Railway train is in the siding. The houses at the top of the right hand side embankment in avenues named after contemporary Liberal politicians are still there. The retaining wall has always been a problem. In the thirties, a concrete raft replaced the buttresses to deal with a land slip. Today the now weathered raft is still there and the wall nearer the camera has, in recent years, been affected by subsidence and replaced by a metal fence.
E.C. Lloyd collection

A view of Leasowe Station in Edwardian days. The main building would appear to be the station master's house with the booking office facilities in the form of a simple lean-to structure. The signal frame can be seen on a simple raised plinth beside the booking office. This would be purely for the operation of the level crossing gates and it is interesting to note that no weather protection was provided for the crossing keeper. *A.M. Rodgers Collection*

A much later view, looking towards Bidston, taken in 1978. The signal box, part of which can just be seen beyond the footbridge, is not a block post controlling a signalling section and its only function is to protect the level crossing. The proposal to change this crossing to automatic barriers has been the cause of much controversy in recent years. The concrete footbridge and the station buildings are typical of the rebuilding carried out at the time of electrification. *E.C. Lloyd Collection*

A busy scene at Moreton Station c1923. The coaches are six-wheeled and are probably gas or oil lit. The main body of passengers appears to be an orphanage outing accompanied by nuns. The grey habits and distinctive whimples of the nuns tell us that they were Daughters of the Charity of St. Vincent de Paul. This Order had orphanages for boys in both Bebington and Liverpool. The nun's headgear was still in use some thirty years later as can be seen from the picture of West Kirby joint station on page 27. The station at this time was still the old Wirral Railway buildings which were somewhat basic. The destination fingerboard shows that the train is going to Birkenhead Park with connections onward to James Street and Liverpool Low Level. A second fingerboard is in the slot at the base of the post and carried the legend 'Seacombe, Liverpool Landing Stage'. Of particular interest is the signal box at right angles to the line. This was replaced by an LMS-built box of LNWR design, on the opposite side of the line.

Ian Boumphrey Collection

Permanent Way gang at Moreton Station, probably before the first World War. They appear to be replacing sleepers. The gentlemen on the platform do not appear to be manual workers and are probably the Station master and the porter who have each borrowed a pick for the benefit of the photographer. The poster board on the left is headed Lancashire and Yorkshire Railway. This railway company did not have direct links with the Wirral network but obviously felt that its services should be advertised on the peninsula.

B.L. Wilson Collection

Photographed on 20th October 1937, a West Kirby bound goods train hauled by ex-LNWR 'Coal Tank' 0-6-2T number 7838 passes Moreton signal box. The small engine is hauling a heavy train and the blast of its exhaust would have been widely heard. Few people today realise how much freight was moved by rail in those days. The train would set down and pick up freight wagons at numerous places on its journey through West Kirby and along the line from there to Hooton, now the Wirral Way. The signal box is still there as, at the time of writing, is the upper quadrant LMS type semaphore signal. In the foreground is an LNW ground or dwarf signal controlling the exit from the station yard. The tower of St. Hilary's Church is just visible on the skyline to the left of the signal box. Today this area is occupied by the Cadbury's factory buildings and the houses on the Leasowe estate. On the right are the houses on the Moreton estate which are now screened by the bushes and trees which have grown to a height of 20 to 30 feet. The shining insulator pots of the recently laid third rail can be seen on the left.
E.C. Lloyd Collection

A view of Meols station from the overbridge looking east towards Moreton. This shows very much the same architectural style as the rebuilt Hoylake Station although rather less ornate. The LMS "hawks eye" nameboard still survived when this photograph was taken in 1951. The signal at the end of the platform was unusually tall in order that the driver of a train coming from West Kirby could see its indication over the top of the road bridge. Beyond the station limits, the featureless landscape has changed little since the railway was built in 1866.
J.N. Barlow Collection

This view of Manor Road Station was taken in the 1960s. However, it still looks much as it did when it was opened in 1941. The signs are of the BR style current at the time with 'totems' on the concrete lamp-posts. These lamp-posts were replaced and the platforms lengthened in the early eighties to accommodate the class 508 trains which were transferred from the Southern Region. *Stations U.K.*

A view of Hoylake Station looking east towards Bidston and Birkenhead, taken in the early years of the present century. A Wirral Railway tank engine is arriving on a train for West Kirby. The Wirral Railway paint shop is visible behind the station buildings on the right hand side. The barrow on the left-hand platform is a curiosity. We do not know its precise use but it seems likely that it was used for conveying mail bags to and from the nearby Post Office. Further down the platform is a train indicator showing that the next train is at 2.20 (14.20 in modern parlance). This indicator had to be re-set manually by the station staff after each train had left. One member of the station staff is very sure that he can beat the train whilst another seems to be performing a balancing act on the platform edge!
E.C. Lloyd Collection

Hoylake Station looking North-West towards the coast before the more recent fire station and Post Office were built. The tracks into the paint shop can be seen in the foreground with the coal yard beyond the station. At the time of writing, the building on the extreme right is the Ming Dynasty Restaurant. In the station yard can be seen the various coal merchants' cabins and several wagons are in the course of being unloaded. Most seem to originate from the North Staffordshire coalfield.
E.C. Lloyd Collection

A view of the exterior of Hoylake Station after the rebuilding which took place when the Wirral lines were electrified in 1937/8. This station is a superb example of the architecture of the period. The footbridge not only gave access to the West Kirby bound platform but also enabled pedestrians to cross the lines when the level crossing gates were closed. Although other stations on the line were reconstructed at the same time, the superior provision at Hoylake indicates that the LMS management acknowledged the social importance of this location.
Ian Boumphrey Collection

West Kirby Station in later Wirral or early LMS days. Wirral signal box and signals are much in evidence. Note that the starting signals for the platform roads are situated by the runround loops and not immediately next to the line they controlled. The signal on the right is off for the train standing in the platform. In the foreground is the double line connection to the joint line to Hooton. The large building behind the station is the YMCA which has long since been demolished; the Abbey National Building Society now occupies that site.
E.C. Lloyd Collection

A similar view in 1938 with an electric set in the sidings and the third rail in position. Electric services started about six weeks later. The starting signals are still one track removed from the roads they serve but they have now been replaced by LNWR arms. The connection to the joint lines is now single and is controlled by upper quadrant signals. The signal box has been replaced - the one just visible on the right hand side is the present box. Although the sidings have all gone and the goods yard replaced by the Concourse, the layout to the right of the platform 1 starter (the signal in the off position) is unchanged other than the lead into the siding on which the electric set is stored.
E.C. Lloyd Collection

A view of the 'concourse' of West Kirby Station. The picture was taken some time between August 1967 - the car has an F registration plate - and 1971 when decimal currency was introduced - indicated by the charge for cycle storage shown on the poster.
E.C. Lloyd Collection

This aerial view of West Kirby shows clearly both the Wirral Railway station and that of the Joint line (top left). The picture would appear to date from the late 1950s. The former Wirral Railway was electrified in 1938 and the Christian Institute, the building opposite the station, was demolished in 1963. The Abbey National office now stands on this site. The sidings nearest to the Wirral station are on the site of the original West Kirby station, opened in 1878. The ridged glass canopy covers the station concourse and survived until the development of the station in 1985/6. Just to the left of this is a small building, latterly used as a store. This building, which also survived until 1985 was part of the original 1878 station. Next comes the coal yard with a solitary coal wagon and, further to the left, the general goods yard which appears to be very much busier. This area is now the site of the West Kirby Concourse. The absence of motor vehicles will be noted as will the queue for the Tudor Cinema on the corner of Bridge Road. The photograph appears to have been taken on a summer evening and one wonders what attractive film programme was tempting so many to the Cinema on such an evening.
E.C. Lloyd Collection

What Time did the Watch Stop?

WIRRAL RAILWAY ATHLETIC CLUB
GRAND
Penny Guessing Competition
FOR A
Gentleman's 18-Carat 22-GUINEA GOLD KEYLESS CENTRE-SECOND HUNTING STOP WATCH

Maker: ARTHUR G. BREWER, Hoylake *(Clock Contractor to the Wirral Railway Co.)*

Committee for the Competition :

S. J. CARR, ESQ., *Chairman.* E. G. BARKER, ESQ., *Vice-Chairman.*

C. E. Adams.	C. Critchlow,	T. Hughes,	T. Molyneux,	T. Smathers,
A. G. Brewer,	G. F. Cherry,	Jas. Johnstone,	A. E. Nash,	Jos. Smith,
J. E. Carr,	J. S. Dawson,	R. L. Jones,	C. Rendell,	Geo. Tottey,
T. Copeland,	W. H. Davies,	C. Mathews,	J. Simpson,	F. W. True.

The object of the Competition is to endeavour to raise sufficient funds to meet the cost of re-building the Pavilion, relaying the Cricket Ground, Boarding in the Field, and putting it in proper repair for the next football season. The Committee sincerely trust you will do your utmost for the welfare of the Club.

Hour.	Minute	Second	Name.	Address.	Hour.	Minute	Second	Name.	Address.
3	26	0	A. Lloyd	Bidston Sidings	,,	,,	30	J. Covall	Bidston
,,	,,	1	A. Lloyd		,,	,,	31	F. Rowe	Wallasey
,,	,,	2	B. Jones	Moreton	,,	,,	32	F. Westcott	Wallasey
,,	,,	3	R. Gibson	Bidston Sidings	,,	,,	33		
,,	,,	4	E. Joynson	Wallasey	,,	,,	34		
,,	,,	5	J. Greenough	Dock Cottages	,,	,,	35		
,,	,,	6	F. Westcott	Wallasey	,,	,,	36		
,,	,,	7	A. Boyle	Bidston Sidings	,,	,,	37		
,,	,,	8	A. Tarr	6 Munster St. B'head	,,	,,	38		
,,	,,	9	J. Greenough	Dock Cottages	,,	,,	39		
,,	,,	10	M. Fawcett	Wallasey	,,	,,	40		
,,	,,	11	J. Greenough	Dock Cottages	,,	,,	41		
,,	,,	12	J. Westcott	Wallasey	,,	,,	42		
,,	,,	13	G. Anderson	Docks Station	,,	,,	43		
,,	,,	14	G. Speed	Bidston Sidings	,,	,,	44		
,,	,,	15	G. Roberts	6 Munster St. B'head	,,	,,	45		
,,	,,	16	G. Anderson	Docks Station	,,	,,	46		
,,	,,	17	J. Parkinson	Bidston	,,	,,	47		
,,	,,	18	A. Lamb	Bidston	,,	,,	48		
,,	,,	19	W. Goddard	432 Beckwith St.	,,	,,	49		
,,	,,	20	H. Davies	Bidston Sidings	,,	,,	50		
,,	,,	21	Wm. Johnson	Bidston Sidings	,,	,,	51		
,,	,,	22	J. Goldsworthy	Bidston	,,	,,	52		
,,	,,	23	J. Westcott	Wallasey	,,	,,	53		
,,	,,	24	W. Johnson	Bidston Sidings	,,	,,	54		
,,	,,	25	J. Covall	Bidston Village	,,	,,	55		
,,	,,	26	J. Parkinson	Bidston	,,	,,	56		
,,	,,	27	W. Bennett	Bidston	,,	,,	57		
,,	,,	28	W. Bennett	Bidston	,,	,,	58		
,,	,,	29	F. Westcott	Wallasey	,,	,,	59		

The Watch to be subscribed for at one penny per line, and will be sold (at his or her own estimate) to the person whose name and address is opposite the exact second at which the watch stops after being sealed up and set at random by H. O. Palfrey, Esq., Manager North & South Wales Bank, New Brighton, who will open on *August 26th, 1897*, and state the exact second it stopped in the presence of six of the Committee, who will then forward it to the successful competitor, whose name and address will be given in the Liverpool evening papers and *Birkenhead News*.

In the event of no name being opposite the exact time at which the Watch stopped it will be given to the nearest estimate, and in case of equalising to the name below. No division of seconds will be taken into account—the hand of the watch having *passed* one second, it will be presumed to be at the next.

All sheets must be returned to the Secretaries not later than August 19th. New sheets can be had from all the Members of the Committee, all Station Masters on the Wirral Railway Co.'s lines, and from the Joint Treasurers and Secretaries.

JAMES OAKES, Graving Dock Hotel, 1, Beaufort Road, Birkenhead.
THOS. JONES, Station Master, Docks Station, Birkenhead.
PERCY J. CARR, New Brighton Station.

These sheets are registered. All applications for their use must be made to "Bazaar," 19, Brunswick Road, Liverpool.

This Wirral railway Athletic Club Competition dates from 1897

Wallasey Village Station looking towards Birkenhead North. The LMS pattern 'Hawks-eye' station nameboard is still in situ which would indicate a date in the late 40s or early 50s before the BR pattern nameboard and lamppost 'totems' were installed.
We are led to believe that the station seen here was reconstructed after the original Wirral Railway station suffered war time bomb damage. The ferro-concrete construction used on the stations rebuilt during electrification was again employed, no doubt with some particular foundation difficulties due to it being sited on an embankment. All our attempts to find a photograph of the original Wirral Railway station have been unsuccessful. Can you help us?
Stations U.K.

The Wirral Railway was always intended to be a local line with regular passengers taking regular journeys. Here it is in operation at Wallasey Village where the 8.20am from New Brighton calls. The regulars, smartly dressed businessmen and long-haired, mini-skirted secretaries, join it. The scene is typical of the early sixties. The wooden platform seats supplied by the LMS in the 1930s were not conducive to passenger comfort. They are still in use but no longer on the Wirral platforms; they now grace the main station of the Llangollen Railway.

J.B. Horne

Wallasey (now Grove Road) Station with a train arriving from New Brighton composed of four wheeled coaches (originally oil lit) hauled by a Wirral Railway 0-4-4T tank engine built by Beyer, Peacock of Manchester. The building is of mock Tudor design and dates from the opening of the line in 1888. This station was renamed Wallasey Grove Road to avoid confusion with the Wallasey Village station. Note the Wirral Horn in the stone feature built into the pediment wall above the bay window. The station structure is little changed today but the clock is no longer in situ. *John Alsop Collection*

Another view of Wallasey (Grove Road) Station looking in the Birkenhead direction. The large enamel advertising signs under the "Wallasey Station" sign are of interest. The pen nibs are by Boon and Blessings whose catch phrase was:

"The Pickwick, the Owl and the Waverley Pen
Come as a boon and a blessing to men."

The Globe Furnishing Company was then a well known shop in Pembroke Place, Liverpool. Bryant and May's Matches encourage us to "Support Home Industries - Employ British Labour." It is somewhat ironic that, during the preparation of this booklet, the closure was announced of the Bryant & Mays factory at Garston, the very last match making factory in Britain.

E.C. Lloyd Collection

Two views from Harrison Drive overbridge just to the north of Grove Road Station which can be seen in the distance. There is little change in the railway scene between the two pictures apart from electrification which dates the second picture as after 1938. The earlier picture is undated but is probably before the first world war. This picture illustrates one of the problems faced by the Wirral Railway, that of drifting sand. The problem seems to have been overcome by the time of the later photograph. Away from the railway itself, changes can be seen, notably the development of Windsor's garage which is very prominent to the left of the later picture.
Upper: E.C. Lloyd Collection; Lower: J.W. Gahan

A 1937 view of the derelict station at Warren which had closed in 1915. In its final years, this station had a service of only one train in each direction on weekdays. On Sundays, a train from New Brighton called in the morning but there was no corresponding service in the opposite direction. The minimal service was finally killed by the tram service along Warren Drive. At the time of the picture, no evidence remained of a platform on the down (New Brighton) line.

E.C. Lloyd Collection

A view of New Brighton Station, looking East, probably taken in the early 1900s. The Tower, seen to the right of St. James" Church spire, opened in 1900 and the open land between Atherton Street and Rowson Street seen to the left of the station building had been developed by 1914. The station building is largely unaltered to-day but a heavy concrete canopy over the platform would now dominate the view. In this picture a Wirral Railway tank locomotive is standing at the head of a short train awaiting departure to either Birkenhead Park or Seacombe. Passing by in Victoria Road is one of the newly introduced tramcars which led to the demise of the Seacombe train service in 1911. An unusual feature evident in this picture is the fence segregating arriving and departing passengers. This is an early example of crowd control at a resort station.　　　　　　　　　　　　　　　　　　　　　　　　　　*E.C. Lloyd Collection*

Another view of New Brighton Station in Wirral Railway days after arrival of a typical train comprising tank engine and an eight coach set of four wheelers. Once again there is a passing tramcar in Victoria Road running on route WD (Warren Drive). Behind the tram is a house once occupied by the General Manager of the railway, next to it is a building then known as the "Assembly Rooms" and next (above the engine) is the then almost new Hotel Victoria. The basket the porter is moving will be theatrical costumes for one of New Brighton's theatres, Winter Gardens, Floral Pavilion or Tivoli, once an important source of traffic. Scenery etc., was loaded into special vans after the shows on Saturday night and left on the 1pm Sunday train to West Kirby to connect with the 1.50pm joint line train probably to Woodside (as there would be no shunter at Hooton on Sunday), thence to its next location. Of interest to railway operating enthusiasts is the two lever ground frame, seen in the left foreground, controlling the engine release cross-over.
E.C. Lloyd Collection

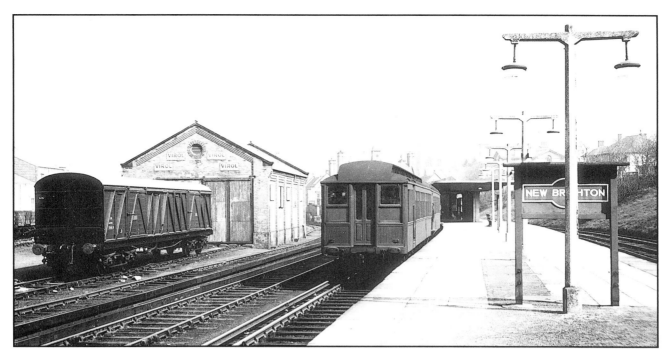

A 1950s view at New Brighton showing a typical scenery van parked outside the goods shed which is well adorned with enamel signs advertising "Virol". A train of ex-Mersey Railway stock awaits departure. After electrification of the Wirral lines in 1938, Mersey Railway stock normally worked the New Brighton and Rock Ferry services on weekdays and operated to West Kirby on Sundays. The station sign is a "Hawks Eye" pattern introduced by the London Midland & Scottish Railway during the 1930s. After nationalisation, British Railways replaced these signs by stove enamel signs called 'totems' which were attached to the station lamp posts. However, New Brighton did not appear to have been provided with BR totems presumably because, it being a terminus, passengers had to leave the train whatever their feelings and if you were departing, you should know where you were anyway.
H.B Priestley/Pacer Archives

A most interesting Edwardian view of the exterior of New Brighton station. Two o'clock in the afternoon was the normal time for the change over of shifts. This probably accounts for the unusually large number of station staff in the line-up. What is very evident is the extent to which the railways were labour intensive in those days. This is in stark contrast to the one-man (or even no-man) operation of many stations today. The prominent sign proclaiming the function of the building would be for the benefit of returning trippers whose vision might have been somewhat impaired by the quantity of refreshment consumed during the day.
Stations U.K.

Trains from New Brighton to Seacombe left the line to Birkenhead North at Seacombe Junction which was originally a triangular junction with a pond in the middle of it and situated on Bidston Moss. The course of the former Seacombe branch is now followed by the approach road to the Kingsway Tunnel. This view is looking towards Seacombe at Slopes Branch Junction where a line branched off to the right to enable freight trains to gain access to the Dock Board's lines. It was used particularly by trains originating from the Chester and Wrexham direction via the Great Central Railway's (later LNER) mid-Wirral line. The Great Central Railway ultimately established a goods depot at Seacombe on Birkenhead Road. Immediately ahead and to the right of the signalbox can be seen a property known latterly as "Darley Dene" but earlier as "Slopes" (hence Slopes Branch). During World War II, the building was occupied by Port Control Officers and was destroyed during an air raid in March 1941.

E.C. Lloyd Collection

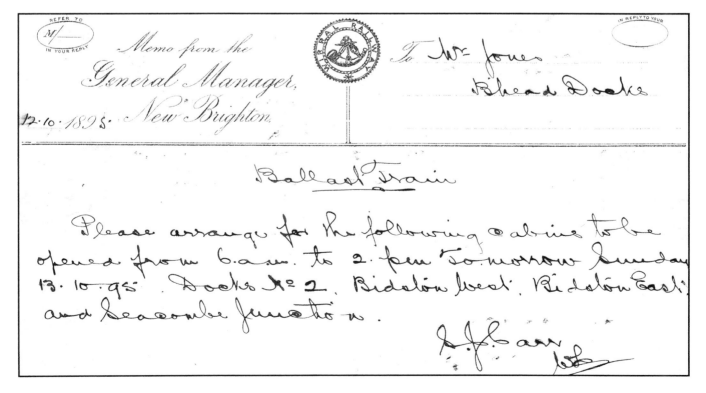

Memo from the General Manager, New Brighton to a Mr Jones at Birkenhead Docks 1895

Regular Kingsway tunnel users will recognise the cutting on the approach to Liscard and Poulton station, which was a modest island platform approached by a covered overbridge leading off the roadway which ran down steeply from Mill Lane bridge to the siding below. This picture shows LMS (ex-LNW) Coal Tank No.7841 leaving with a train for West Kirby on 12th February 1938. Signals and the crossover visible in the foreground were controlled from the signal box at the Slopes Branch Junction. The siding was used mainly for domestic coal which would be bagged by local merchants and hauled away, originally by horses, up the sloping approach road for delivery. The railings on the left of the picture bound a pathway which led to steps in the sandstone leading up to Breck Road.
E.C. Lloyd Collection

A view from the platform end at Liscard & Poulton station, looking towards Breck road bridge and showing the coal siding. The points for the siding were controlled from a ground frame in the small cabin at the foot of the platform ramp but under the overall control of Slopes Branch Junction signal box. This signal box, which can just be seen beyond Breck Road bridge, also controlled the main line signals at this station. Older readers will be able to visualise the wonderful "sea green" livery of the Wallasey Corporation bus passing over the bridge.
I.W. Anderson

In LMS days a train from West Kirby is seen approaching Seacombe Station hauled by Stanier 2-6-2T No.159. The stock is a former LNWR three coach set strengthened by the addition of an LMS non corridor coach. The building on the right is the location of the present Kwik Save store in Church Road. The cutting has now been filled in but the bridge stonework can still be seen at the far end of the Kwik Save car park.
E.C. Lloyd Collection

This is probably the same train as shown in the previous picture but seen here in Seacombe Station after the engine has run round its coaches. The station here retained its "temporary" corrugated iron buildings throughout its life from 1895 until closure on 4th January 1960. It was originally intended to build a more impressive station, unified with the ferry terminal, but this never materialised. At night it was a dimly lit place with platform illumination provided by gas lamps. This is in stark contrast to the illumination provided at Wallasey's other railway terminus at New Brighton. Seacombe Station was used by trains from New Brighton (up to 1911), West Kirby (until March 1938), and Wrexham until closure in 1960.
E.C. Lloyd Collection

An LMS design 2-6-2T at the buffer stops at Seacombe Station probably in the course of running round its train. The clock tower of the Seacombe Ferry Terminal is a prominent feature of the scene. *M.H. Walshaw/Courtesy Hugh Davies*

As a railway terminus, few station frontages, if any, can match this for unprepossessing appearance and attraction. Even after nationalisation, the powers that be decided to retain its archaic glory. Reference is made to trains to New Brighton. By the time that this picture was taken, through services to the neighbouring resort were a thing of the distant past. By now, such a journey would entail two changes of train, at Bidston and at Birkenhead North. Buses running direct to New Brighton ran from the ferry terminal across the road! Protruding from the top of the notice board is not a decorative station finial but the spire of St. Paul's Church. The white building to the right was not part of the station but Fred's Cafe, well patronised by those who appreciated a good mug of tea and quality 'nosh'. *J.F. Ward Collection*

Chapter Three
THE MERSEY RAILWAY

Wirral's next railway was one it shared with Liverpool. The attraction of Wirral as a dormitory for Liverpool businessmen had long been recognised with the need for improved cross-river communication becoming increasingly acute.

On 20th January 1886, the Mersey Railway was opened between Liverpool James Street and Green Lane, Tranmere with two intermediate stations in Birkenhead, Hamilton Square and Central. The crucial branch to Birkenhead Park, in order to connect with the Wirral Railway's network of lines, was established in February 1888. In the same year the extension from Green Lane to Rock Ferry enabled passengers to connect easily with the Joint Line's services between Woodside and Chester. The Mersey Railway paid passenger tolls for the privilege of using the LNW - GW Joint Station at Rock Ferry.

1892 saw the opening of the final part of the Mersey Railway, the section from James Street to the Low Level Station at Liverpool Central. Here the Station was owned by the Mersey Railway, although the ownership of the site remained with the Cheshire Lines Committee whose trains ran into the High Level Station.

At this time the Mersey Railway used steam locomotives on a line which featured, in the tunnel rising from under the river, the most severe gradient for a passenger line in Britain. The intention was to descend on a gradient of 1 in 30 on either side, but the discovery of a pre-glacial rock fault on the Liverpool side necessitated a realignment of 1 in 27!

The Mersey Railway was now complete but was soon in financial difficulties. Whilst the journey under the river was rather quicker than using the ferries, for passengers asphyxiation in a smoke filled tunnel was scarcely an improvement, or an acceptable alternative to being tossed about on a Mersey ferry boat by gales which could occur at any time of the year in this part of the country.

By 1887, the company was in receivership. Indeed, in 1902, the receipts failed to cover the operating costs, let alone contribute to the interest on the capital which had been borrowed to build the line.

Mindful of the success of electric underground railways in London, the operating Board commissioned a report on the feasibility of electrifying the railway. The consultants report was in favour and stated that the line could be electrified for "about £70,000". Even if this were true, the company did not have this amount of money, still less did it have the £635,000 it actually cost to electrify.

George Westinghouse, the American industrialist, had established a works in England at Trafford Park in Manchester and was looking for business. He offered to electrify the railway as a 'showcase' for his company's products and the contract was signed in July 1901. The only way the Receiver could pay him was to offer Debenture Stock which Westinghouse accepted.

Under the terms of the agreement, electrification had to be carried out without interfering with the steam working. All the electrical equipment, including the generating sets, had to be brought from America. At midnight on 2nd May 1903, the last steam train left Liverpool Central and, at 4.53am the following day, the first electric train entered the same station. The weekday service was operated on that Sunday although the public were not admitted until noon when the Sunday service would normally start. This stands in stark contrast to today's experiences. As George Westinghouse had predicted, electrification of the Mersey line brought about a complete transformation in cross-river travel and also in the Company's fortunes.

Originally a freight line spur to connect with the Liverpool Docks had been planned and the heading for this is still detectable on the left hand side as one enters the Liverpool Loop from Birkenhead. This spur was never completed and the line was solely passenger carrying, with the Company maintaining its independence even after the 1923 grouping of railway companies and up until nationalisation of all of Britain's railways on 1st January 1948. On the other hand the Wirral Railway and the London and North Western Railway companies became part of the London, Midland and Scottish Railway Company in 1923.

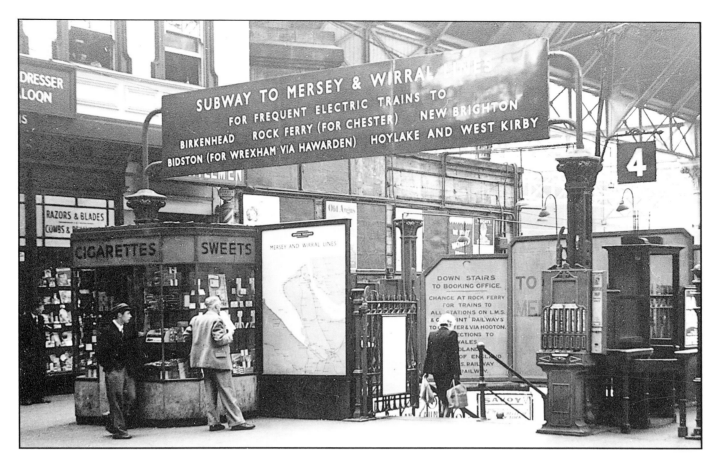

Not a Wirral Station it's true but this was the gateway to the Wirral for many people. This is Liverpool Central and shows the entrance to the subway to the Low Level Station of the Mersey Railway. The board above and the map to the left of the steps, says it all. The platforms to which the steps lead no longer serve Wirral Line trains but those of the Northern Line to Hunts Cross, Southport, Ormskirk and Kirkby. Present day trains to Wirral run very much deeper underground.
J.N. Barlow Collection

At James Street Station, Liverpool, the full title is emblazoned on the wall. Note the semaphore signal which permitted trains to reverse direction here and cross over to return to Birkenhead. Interestingly, the railway has at this stage been electrified but the station appears to retain gas lighting and the signal has an oil lamp!
E.C. Lloyd Collection

An old view of the hydraulic tower at Hamilton Square Station. The station entrance is modest in comparison with the ornate brickwork to the Italianate tower. Presumably the Mersey Railway's architect felt obliged to emulate the splendour of the adjacent Square. One well known writer described how going up to street level in one of the "ponderous old hydraulic lifts (which he claimed were bigger than many a station waiting room) was a slow and dignified process, and through a grid in the ceiling could be seen the massive chains and wheels of the hydraulic gear leading to a sort of twilight in the lift-tower." The first electric lifts were installed at James Street in 1938 as part of the modernisation related to the electrification of the Wirral lines. At the time, they were claimed to be the largest in the country operating at such high speed and, after proving themselves, a similar installation followed at Hamilton Square.

E.C. Lloyd Collection

Platform level at Hamilton Square c1910 which would have been dimly lit by the incandescent gas lighting of the period. Note the preferential treatment offered to first class passengers who are advised where to wait by means of a projecting sign.

E.C. Lloyd Collection

A view of Birkenhead Central Station showing the original footbridge which was situated mid-way along the platform and provided a direct exit to Argyle Street South, adjacent to the Head Offices of the Railway. To the right of the platforms are the original car sheds which were later extended as traffic increased and more rolling stock became necessary. Signals and signalling equipment on the Mersey Railway were provided by the Railway Signal Co. of Fazakerley.

E.C. Lloyd Collection

Birkenhead Central station overbridge under reconstruction in 1930. On the left hand side of the photograph is the line to Hamilton Square and Liverpool whilst on the right, part of a coach can be discerned in the Mersey Railway carriage sidings. Photographic details provide a fascinating insight into contemporary workman's apparel, tools, equipment and construction methods. The structure was erected in 1885 by the Birkenhead firm of J. Gordon Alison & Co. and reconstructed by the same firm in 1930. Apart from the "Keep to the Right" notices, the structure has remained intact and the recent repainting by Merseyrail commendably highlights the spandrels and cast iron decorative detail.

C.E. Heywood Collection

With the four rail Mersey Railway electrification system very evident, this rare view of the interior of Green Lane station depicts the stark functionalism of its platforms. Having emerged from the tunnel into the station platform, travellers glimpsed daylight through the overhead station cover. Even so, the platform edges have been painted white to assist passengers. The rear of a Mersey Railway train departing for Rock Ferry is visible as it emerges into full daylight and fresh air. A brave attempt has been made to brighten the surroundings with 1930s advertisements. The station was opened in 1886 and caters for the inhabitants of Lower Tranmere and, in recent times, for passengers arriving by road and parking their cars on the adjacent car park. At one time when the nearby Cammell Laird shipyard was in full production, it handled a great surge of passengers at the start and finish of each working day. Note the shelter, providing respite for the few from the draughts which were very prevalent at this station.
Ken Longbottom Collection

An early Mersey Railway scene at Rock Ferry showing a steam hauled train arriving from Liverpool hauled by a "condensing" tank locomotive. These were designed to reduce steam emission in the tunnels since the exhaust steam from the cylinders was transferred via the large diameter pipe into the water tank rather than to atmosphere via the chimney as on a normal locomotive. Signals and signalbox are of standard LNWR pattern.
E.C. Lloyd Collection

Interesting comparisons can be made between the previous view and this similar one of Rock Ferry taken in 1956, looking in the same direction. Some LNWR signals still survived and can be seen in the background. The signals on the platform ends have been replaced by LMS upper quadrant types which are at varying heights in contrast to the LNW ones which afforded all routes equal status. A British Railways standard design signalbox has just rendered the LNWR one redundant. Also facing redundancy is the electric train set passing the box which is of the Westinghouse American pattern and about to be replaced by new stock based on the LMS pattern introduced onto the West Kirby and New Brighton lines when they were electrified in 1938.
J.A. Peden

An Edwardian view at Birkenhead Park with smartly attired passengers obviously awaiting their Wirral Railway train after disembarking from the adjacent Mersey Railway electric train with its distinctive American design stock. Note the family group complete with picnic basket. Park Station was originally an independent station managed by a joint committee representing both railways. The station staff were employed by the committee and provided with uniforms with distinctive buttons and cap badges. The station was an interchange point until the LMS introduced through electric services in 1938. The main building seen on the overbridge was destroyed by enemy action in 1941. The signal box was of Mersey Railway pattern and was designated Cabin "H", being reconstructed in the same location by the LMS in 1938. This second box was demolished in 1988 following simplification of track layout and resignalling.
E.C. Lloyd Collection

Chapter Four
THE NORTH WALES and LIVERPOOL RAILWAY

The final development in the creation of Wirral's railway network was a further joint venture designed to gain access to Birkenhead Docks and was promoted jointly by the Manchester, Sheffield and Lincolnshire Railway and the Wrexham, Mold and Connah's Quay Railway. The lines of the two companies met at Dee Marsh near the present Shotton Steelworks, and a line was built and opened in 1896 which ran down the centre of Wirral to a junction at Bidston. Intermediate stations were built at Neston, Barnston (later Storeton for Barnston) and Upton. Prior to opening, this joint undertaking had various titles at different times but it opened in 1896 as the North Wales and Liverpool Railway. This name lasted less than nine years as the line was absorbed by the Great Central Railway on 1st January 1905.

In the meantime stations had been opened at Heswall Hills on 1st May 1898 and Burton Point on 1st August 1899. In the railway grouping of 1923 the Great Central Railway became part of the London and North Eastern Railway Company.

Passenger services were of minor importance and this was, in no small measure, due to the fact that some of the stations were remote from the communities they purported to serve. However, the company did provide regular passenger services between Seacombe and both Chester (Northgate Station) and Wrexham using the Wirral Railway's (later LMSR) line from Seacombe to Bidston.

A transitional scene at Bidston in the early 1960s with a well patronised diesel multiple unit service bound for New Brighton. These trains, which operated to and from Chester, Shotton and Wrexham, replaced the steam services when Seacombe closed in 1960. The service to Chester was especially popular with Saturday shoppers from Wallasey but ended when Chester Northgate station closed in 1968. The threat of closure also hung over the Wrexham service for a while until reprieved by the Minister of Transport in 1969, by which time Upton and Heswall stations had become unmanned. The Wrexham service was subsequently diverted to terminate at Birkenhead North from January 1971 but this often caused disruption to the electric services, particularly during the peak periods. The present arrangement of terminating Wrexham services at Bidston was introduced in October 1978.

Stations on the mid-Wirral line of the former Great Central Railway (later LNER), which ran from Bidston Dee Junction to Wrexham, were in two distinct architectural styles. The simpler of the two is displayed here at Upton with its large booking hall on the overbridge and sturdy brick waiting rooms at platform level. A train is signalled in the Bidston direction although the staff appear to be poised for action on the other platform.
H.J. Leadbetter Collection

A view taken from a train standing in the Wrexham bound platform at Upton looking back towards Bidston further illustrating the style of buildings. Note the lamp casings in which paraffin lamps would be inserted as darkness approached. Note also the flower beds at the booking office end of the platform and the sandstone shaft behind the trees which is still a local landmark. This structure was originally part of the old Ford waterworks which stood on the site until it fell into disuse in the 1920s.
The late H.C. Casserley/courtesy R.M. Casserley

A view of Storeton (for Barnston) station at the turn of the century with a group of cyclists, who had probably been exploring the rural lanes of Wirral, awaiting their homeward train which is arriving from the Upton direction. Storeton was of similar layout and design to Upton, except that the goods yard and signal box were on the other side of the road bridge (behind the camera). The bridge seen in this view is a farmer's "occupation" bridge which the railway company were required to provide when their lines divided a farm in two. This particular one had access ramps in both directions and must have been an expensive facility to provide considering the close proximity of the road bridge. The date of the demolition of the occupation bridge is not known.

Glyn Parry Collection

Geography dictated an alternative approach at Heswall Hills where the brick built booking hall was at road level and the waiting rooms on the embankment were of timber construction to reduce weight. The platform structures with their covered approach stairways offered protection and substance in stark contrast to what is available to present day travellers. Note that, although the National Grid power lines are alongside, the station is still lit by oil lamps!

J.F. Ward Collection

On Saturday 6th August 1966 the Locomotive Club of Great Britain organised an "enthusiasts' special" comprising nine goods brake vans hauled by an LMS designed "Crab" 2-6-0 No.42942. The train is shown here at Heswall Hills, further illustrating the timber construction of the platforms and buildings. The "Hundred of Wirral" tour ran from Birkenhead to Chester via Hooton and returned via Mickle Trafford and the mid Wirral line to Bidston, thence via the dock lines back to Birkenhead. The train was originally planned to depart from the old terminus at Monks Ferry, but at the last minute the Civil Engineer had misgivings and departure was from Woodside.

B. Taylor

Whilst the emphasis of this book is on passenger stations, the mid-Wirral Line is best remembered by railway enthusiasts for the impressive climbing of Storeton Bank by the British Railways standard class 9F, 2-10-0 locomotives hauling heavy iron ore trains from Bidston Dock to Shotwick Sidings for John Summers' Steel Works. One of these trains is depicted here spreading a spectacular exhaust over Heswall Hills signal box.

Ian Boumphrey Collection

A Great Central rail motor standing in Neston & Parkgate Station. The similarity between the architecture and that in the picture of Upton Station (page 59) will be noted. Rail motors were introduced on many railways in the early years of the present century. The coach body concealed a small steam engine (in this case, at the end nearest the camera) whilst the remainder was taken up by an open saloon for passengers. These machines had several defects, the major one being that, at times of heavy traffic, they could not cope with the extra passengers. If an extra coach was attached, the little engine would be very much overloaded. As a result, they did not last very long although one did survive on the Lancashire & Yorkshire section of the LMS until nationalisation - just!
E.C.Lloyd Collection

At Burton Point the platforms were in a cutting and the buildings were in the more elaborate style with overhanging canopies to the waiting rooms and ornate fretting to the woodwork on the gable of the booking hall. The main brickwork was yellow with red band courses and quoin features - a little garish, perhaps, for this remote country location. This view is after closure and the platform edge copings have been turned back for ease of maintenance.
H.J.Leadbetter

Chapter Five
THE COMPLETED NETWORK
IT'S IMPACT and SUBSEQUENT CHANGES

By the turn of the century, the pattern of railways had had a profound effect on the development and appearance of the Wirral peninsula. The railway network served two distinct purposes, freight and passenger carrying. The freight traffic concentrated on the docks and goods for export together with servicing two large firms, Lever Bros. and the Cammell Laird shipyard, both of which had internal rail systems. The passenger traffic was directed primarily towards Liverpool, the commercial heart of the area.

Despite this progress, an editorial in the Birkenhead News for Saturday 2nd December 1922, which anticipated the forthcoming railway grouping, described the current railways scene as follows:- "The Wirral area has probably one of the most roundabout sets of railway lines to be found anywhere in the country with the result that, not only are travel distances out of all proportion to actual distances but, until the advent of the motor bus, important villages were without any means of communication except by ordinary wheeled vehicle or on foot". The editorial then cites the situation at West Kirby as a typical transport hiatus. "Sooner or later, and the sooner the better, the new management would have to get rid of the absolutely anomalous state of things existing at West Kirby where two lines come each to a dead end almost side by side instead of being united to form a continuous service. Every consideration of common sense and convenience point to the linking up of these two sections of the line and to the desirability, in the course of time, of doubling the section between West Kirby and Hooton". It is regrettable that this opportunity, so obvious to the editor, was ignored by the "new management".

Another editorial, on Wednesday 6th December 1922, discussed further "necessary improvements" expected after the grouping of the railway companies. These improvements included :- a) Relaying to LNWR standards of the permanent way from Birkenhead Park to New Brighton and from West Kirby to Seacombe. b) electrification of the system by 1st July 1923. c) construction of a terminus worthy of it's location at Seacombe. a) and b) were eventually achieved in 1938 when the electrification of the lines from Birkenhead Park to West Kirby and New Brighton enabled the through running of passenger trains to Liverpool, but c) remained a pious aspiration.

Notwithstanding the challenge of road transport from the 1920s onwards, the railways continued to play a vital role in people's lives until well after the Second World War. Since the 1960s the railways have steadily lost the battle for freight and passenger traffic but, despite the consequences of various economic axes wielded by Dr. Beeching and his successors, the railway map of Wirral has remained largely intact.

On Wirral's first railway from Birkenhead to Chester trains now travel through the tunnel of the former Mersey Railway from Liverpool en route to Chester. Birkenhead Town station closed in 1945 to be followed by Ledsham (1959), Mollington (1960) and Woodside (1967). In 1969 because of the decline in freight traffic the section of line from Ledsham Junction to Rock Ferry reverted to two tracks. By 1985 electrification of the line from Rock Ferry to Hooton was completed and this continued through to Chester in 1993. A new station opened at Bromborough Rake between Bromborough and Spital in 1985.

The branch lines from Hooton experienced mixed fortunes. The line to West Kirby closed completely in 1963 although closure to passengers had occurred as follows: Thurstaston, Caldy and Kirby Park in 1954 followed by Hadlow Road (Willaston), Neston South, Parkgate and Heswall in 1955. Most of the former trackbed is now the Wirral Way Country Park. The line to Helsby has fared much better. Passenger use has increased to such an extent that a new station was opened at Overpool, between Little Sutton and Ellesmere Port, in 1988 and electrification to Ellesmere Port was completed in 1994.

The former Wirral Railway lines have experienced one significant alteration. Liscard and Poulton station, together with the branch terminus at Seacombe, closed to passengers in 1960. In 1971 the trackbed was used to form the approach road from the M53 motorway to a second Mersey road tunnel connecting Wallasey to Liverpool. The only other closure on Wirral's second railway occurred in 1915 when Warren station, adjacent to Warren Drive and between New Brighton and Wallasey (Grove Road) closed on 1st October.

The mid-Wirral line still operates, although the need for interchange at Bidston makes its links more tenuous. Not surprisingly the isolated stations at Storeton and Burton Point closed in 1951 and 1955 respectively. Diesel powered passenger trains still run between Bidston and Wrexham but the site of the former Northgate station at Chester has been converted to a sports and recreational arena. The Mersey Railway has changed significantly with the completion of the Liverpool loop line and a burrowing junction at Hamilton Square in 1977. In transport terms, its progressive link-up with the Wirral lines and, more recently, the electrified lines between Rock Ferry and Chester, has achieved one of the main aims of the original railway promoters - rapid transit to the heart of Liverpool.

EPILOGUE

This book has been compiled by members of the Merseyside Railway History Group which was formed in 1977 as a result of a Workers Education Association course on researching railway history. The course tutor was Dr. David Halsall of Edge Hill College, Ormskirk, who is now the Group's President.

The members involved were:- Jack Barlow, Malcolm Docherty, Charles Heywood, Harry Leadbetter, Edward (Ted) Lloyd, Tim Pestell, Alec Rodgers and Don Wildbore. Messrs. Heywood, Leadbetter and Lloyd have had editorial responsibilities and must take the blame for any errors which have crept in!

Researching railway history is a mainly pleasurable, but sometimes frustrating, activity and much tea and cakes have been consumed at members' homes in this quest. We are indebted to the wives concerned for their forbearance. One particular frustration of this work has been our inability to locate a picture of Wallasey Village station prior to it's rebuilding in the 1940s. We have also been unable to locate good copies of the "official" Wirral Railway photographs of certain stations taken by Arthur Shaw of Seacombe. Can you help?

AND FINALLY . . .

Hardy souls who have completed their walk along the Wirral Way would find it difficult to identify with this view at Hooton. The picture was taken from the brake van of a freight train leaving for West Kirby in 1962. Changes in the railway scene in subsequent years have seen the end of steam traction, the demolition of the magnificent Hooton South Signal Box and the elimination of semaphore signals. All that now remains of this scene is the trackbed - and that is considerably overgrown.

H.J. Leadbetter